NEW VIRTUAL FIELD TRIPS

NEW VIRTUAL FIELD TRIPS

Gail Cooper
and
Garry Cooper

2001
Libraries Unlimited
A Member of Greenwood Publishing, Inc.
Westport, Connecticut • London

Libraries Unlimited
A member of Greenwood Publishing Group, Inc.
88 Post Road West,
Westport, CT 06881
www.lu.com

Library of Congress Cataloging-in-Publication Data

Cooper, Gail, 1950-
    New virtual field trips / Gail Cooper and Garry Cooper.
        p. cm.
    Rev. ed. of: Virtual field trips. 1997.
    Includes bibliographical references and index.
    ISBN 1-56308-887-8 (softbound)
    1. Internet in education--United States. 2. World Wide Web. 3. School field trips--United States. I. Cooper, Garry. II. Cooper, Gail, 1950- Virtual field trips. III. Title.

LB1044.87 .C67 2001
025.04--dc21
                                                        00-045091

10 9 8 7 6 5 4 3 2   IBT   05 04 03

*To Jeff Markunas, Jim F. Markunas, and Palatine High School;
to Alexandra Naomi Cooper, who still loves to learn; to the staff
and teachers of Oliver Wendell Holmes School in Oak Park,
who impress us almost every day.*

Contents

Introduction

Imagine taking your students on a field trip without worrying about procuring transportation, finding chaperones, collecting fees and permission slips, and worrying about weather or lost and wandering children. Now, imagine such a trip completely unconstrained by the boundaries of time and place. That's how we've conceived *New Virtual Field Trips*, and even teachers new to the Internet will find getting on the virtual bus easier than the old-fashioned trips. Our goal in writing *New Virtual Field Trips* is not only to let you know about the myriad learning experiences that are waiting for you and your students, but also to make it easy for you to get there. We've gone on each of these trips ourselves and checked thoroughly for appropriateness. And wait till you see what we've found!

Thanks to the Internet, you can take learning beyond the confines of the classroom. Museums, libraries, schools, and modern and ancient cities around the world have opened their virtual doors and are waiting for your class to arrive. You can take your students to foreign countries, to the bottom of the ocean, and to the farthest reaches of outer space. You can spend an entire day with Thomas Jefferson at Monticello, visit families in African villages and cities, view the Seven Wonders of the Ancient World, meet famous authors, spend a winter at Valley Forge, tour the castles of Europe and Asia, sail the seven seas with pirates, swim with sharks and dolphins, and participate in the Civil War. The world's top laboratories, such as Los Alamos and Fermilab, have their virtual doors open, and their scientists are waiting to share their high-tech equipment and knowledge with your students. Take your class to Broadway theater productions; travel through the human body; listen to the voices of whales and presidents; visit other schools and classrooms; view breathtaking photos from the Hubble telescope; and take chess, piano, art, and calligraphy lessons.

Unlike movies and books, the Internet is interactive. Your students can ask scientists, astronauts, mathematicians, and explorers questions; conduct online frog dissections; participate in real-time discussions with students and professionals around the world; and collaborate on musical compositions, prose and poetry, and artwork with other classes. Best of all, many of the sites are regularly updated, so you can visit over and over and keep on top of the latest developments.

It's been only two years since *Virtual Field Trips* was published, but there's been a world of change. The sounds, animations, videos, and new ideas for teaching and interacting that used to work with only the most up-to-date computers are now available to most of you, and you'll find that the old, familiar virtual field trips, as well as the new ones we've added (over a hundred) now include several of these new features. (If your computer still doesn't have the necessary software, don't worry: Most of our sites tell you how to download the software for free.) In response to your requests, we've added more trips that tie into National Science Standards, utilize inquiry-based learning, and encourage independent studies. We've added more student-written sites, so that your students (and staff) can see the powerful, educational, and creative ways that the Internet can be used by your own school. We've also identified those sites specifically oriented to primary grades. And as usual, we've literally triple-checked each site so that we can give you the most up-to-date and accurate descriptions of what you'll find on your virtual field trips.

How to Use This Book

Think of *New Virtual Field Trips* as a carefully annotated guidebook, arranged by subject matter. Because so many of the places you'll visit cover a variety of subjects, we've extensively cross-referenced our listings. We urge you to use not only the table of contents, but our index as well. We're confident that among our organization, cross-references, and index, you're sure to find at least one, and usually more, field trips that not only suit your needs, but expand your ideas for teaching. Teachers and parents have told us that because of the clear organization of *Virtual Field Trips*, they have recommended it to students for independent research and homework. Students who merely go to the usual Internet sites (the electronic equivalent of using *Encyclopaedia Britannica* or *World Book*) or who enter keywords in a search engine and come up with literally hundreds of possibilities of varying quality and integrity are not maximally benefiting from the Internet's tremendous potential. You can feel safe having your students turn to *New Virtual Field Trips* for research ideas. Our sites will challenge and stimulate them, promote independent and creative thinking, and present information that goes beyond textbook basics. We urge teachers who are looking for ways to freshen or expand lesson plans to use *New Virtual Field Trips* in this same way. And be sure to check *More Virtual Field Trips* for additional topics and tours.

Some basic things haven't changed since *Virtual Field Trips*. Our goal from the beginning has been to help teachers and students use the Internet in ways that make their teaching and learning more efficient, exciting, and educational. *Virtual Field Trips* makes it easy for you to find the resources that fit and supplement your lesson plans and curriculum. Sites with primary grade materials are identified with the symbol **PG**. These are sites geared specifically toward the youngest students. However, be sure to check other sites because many have material suitable for the primary grades. We have made every effort to include such sites in the index. As always, we've gone on each of the trips ourselves several times, selecting only those trips that we think have something to offer beyond the standard Internet fare.

Remember that the Internet is extremely dynamic, and sites often change content. That is one of its great advantages over textbooks and audiovisual aids. However, this also means that our descriptions of each field trip may not exactly match what you'll find when you visit the site. Therefore, if our descriptions of specific exhibits or features seem close to what you're looking for, but not right on target, you may still wish to visit the site. This is especially true with museums and art galleries. Just as with physical museums and galleries, online exhibits change. We suggest that once you find a museum or gallery that seems interesting, bookmark it on your Web browser and check back every few months.

COMMON PROBLEMS

Occasionally, you may find yourself confronted with a message that says, in effect, that the site is closed. This may occur for several reasons, none of which is your fault (unless you've typed an address incorrectly). The site may be temporarily closed for maintenance or updating, it may have moved, or, in rare instances, it may no longer accept visitors. Before you go home disappointed, try this: Retype the address, eliminating segments of the address one by one,

xvi How to Use This Book

from right to left (going backwards toward the beginning). For example, if you can't connect to *http://astro.uchicago.edu/cara/vtour*, eliminate "vtour". If you still can't connect, eliminate "cara". If you manage to connect this way, you may end up in a portion of the site that is different from what is described in *New Virtual Field Trips*. It's like sneaking into a museum through a service entrance. Once you're in, start wandering around, and if you don't find your way to exactly what you've been searching for, you will likely find a serendipitous surprise that also fits your needs.

Occasionally, an address may completely change. Remember to check Libraries Unlimited's Web site (http://www.lu.com), where we will post updates as listings change.

LET US KNOW

Just as many of the virtual field trips are interactive, this book can be seen as an interactive experience as well. You are one of our most important resources. As you wander around the world on your virtual field trips, you may find changes, additions, and deletions, as well as exciting new places. We encourage you to contact us with any ideas, requests, problems, or new field trips that you've discovered. You can e-mail us at either **gailc1@ix.netcom.com** or **gcoop@ix.netcom.com**. We're looking forward to hearing from you and we thank you for your past responses.

CHAPTER 1

VIRTUAL TIME MACHINE

Why just read about people and events, when you can step into the time machine and *experience* some of the greatest events in history? Spend a day with Thomas Jefferson, participate in the *Amistad* revolt, or explore the Seven Wonders of the Ancient World. After fighting in every major war that the United States has been involved in and sailing with pirates, you may wish to relax and spend a day with the Negro Baseball Leagues—if you're not too tired from hanging out at the Ancient Olympics and playing ball with the Mayans.

A-BOMB MUSEUM
http://www.csi.ad.jp/ABOMB

A visit to this Japanese site will provide accurate information about the impact of the atomic bomb on Hiroshima and Nagasaki. The tour is intended to "provide a context for constructive discussion of what the world can learn" to ensure that such weapons of destruction are never used again. To that end, the tour includes eyewitness accounts from children, exhibits from the Peace Memorial Museum, and voices of survivors. There are letters from the mayor of Hiroshima and other Japanese who insist that they have a responsibility not merely to offer themselves as victims, but also to air their own atrocities. The letters from Americans span the range from apologetic to insisting that if Japan had developed the atomic bomb first, *they* would surely have used it. Although the anti-nuclear weaponry bias of the site administrators is clearly stated, they have conscientiously presented all sides of the arguments for and against the use of the atomic bomb.

AFRICAN AMERICAN HISTORY

See also United States—1968 and Chapter 13—King, Doctor Martin Luther, Jr.

Afro American Newspaper Company's History Museum

http://www.afroam.org/index.html

The Afro-American Newspaper Company of Baltimore hosts this multiple decade tour of its *Black History Museum*, beginning with first-hand accounts from slaves who fought and killed for freedom. Students can then travel forward in time to the 1930s and experience "southern justice" while attending the trial of the Scottsboro Boys. The continuing struggle for civil rights is followed through interactive exhibits on Jackie Robinson, the Black Panther Party, and the Million Man March. Other topics include World War II's Tuskegee Airmen and *This Is Our War*—a compilation of articles by African American correspondents such as Ollie Steward and Elizabeth Williams—who reported on African American troops from World War II battlefronts. The *Kid's Zone* presents information about Africa in child-friendly formats such as illustrated myths and puzzles.

American Slave Narratives

http://xroads.virginia.edu/~HYPER/wpa/wpahome.html

The University of Virginia has compiled first-hand accounts of experiences of nineteenth-century slaves from interviews conducted by writers and journalists from the 1936–1938 Works Project Administration. The written and audio narratives powerfully convey the daily lives, work, joys, miseries, and beliefs of more than 2,300 former slaves. An introduction to the tour advises people how to read or hear the narratives, listening for dramatic details so matter-of-factly conveyed that readers might miss them. For example, although Tempe Durham's master hosted a party to celebrate her marriage to Exter Durham, he sent her husband to a different plantation the following day. Joseph Holmes says that he was "always treated fine" because his mistress was raising slaves for the market.

The *Amistad*

http://amistad.mysticseaport.org/main/welcome.html

Mystic Seaport Museum hosts this tour of the *Amistad*—the revolt of 49 Africans led by Cinque that ended in a trial before the United States Supreme Court. Over 500 primary source documents help students to explore the issues, implications, and ramifications of the revolt, while experiencing the political climate of the United States, Cuba, and West Africa through the eyes of the slaves, abolitionists, politicians, and Supreme Court justices. Teachers should be aware that these documents reflect the ideology and beliefs of the times, and many are rather disturbing. Before taking your students on the tour, check the curriculum section for ideas that can be implemented in one or two class periods, including lesson plans for exploring the incident as a political issue, mock trials, debates, and role playing.

Duke University Special Collections Library

http://odyssey.lib.duke.edu/slavery

The *Third Person, First Person: Slave Voices* exhibit at this Duke University site examines the life experiences of American slaves from the late eighteenth through the nineteenth century with details that bring the slavery experience into sharp focus. There are invoices and shipping orders for slaves, first-person accounts, and letters from plantation owners.

Encyclopaedia Britannica's Guide to Black History

http://www.blackhistory.eb.com

Encyclopaedia Britannica's *Guide to Black History* explores five distinct eras—from slavery to modern times—through videos, text, and photographs. Although some of the texts are rather lean, the multimedia exhibits—such as movies of the 1963 clash between civil rights demonstrators and police in Birmingham (with a voice-over by President Kennedy); Hank Aaron's address to Congress; speeches by Malcolm X, Dr. Martin Luther King Jr., and Jesse Jackson; performances by Billie Holiday, Dizzie Gillespie, and Charlie Parker; and Jesse Owen's victory at the 1936 Berlin Olympics—should not be missed.

Harlem: 1900–1940

http://www.si.umich.edu/CHICO/Harlem

Pay a visit to Harlem, the United States' most vibrant urban breeding ground for African American art, music, literature, politics, and business. This tour, hosted by Cultural Heritage Initiatives for Community Outreach (CHICO) at the University of Michigan's School of Information, introduces your students to the people and institutions that put Harlem on the world map. Stop in at a wedding, meet Sarah Breedlove (a poor orphan from Louisiana whose beauty products empire made her one of the country's richest Black women), watch the New York Black Yankees play, and meet some of the greatest jazz artists and writers of the twentieth century. Harlem's a sprawling, vibrant neighborhood, so to efficiently plan your visit, you'll want to check out the teacher's area for lesson plans and strategies.

Library of Congress—African American Mosaic

http://lcweb.loc.gov/exhibits/african/intro.html

Take a trip through 500 years of African American experiences in the Western Hemisphere, from colonization to abolition, migration, and the Works Project Administration. Experiences of this kind convey reality far beyond that gained from textbooks. There is a great deal of material for stimulating classroom discussions and debates on subjects such as the conflicts between abolitionists and slave owners.

National Civil Rights Museum

http://www.mecca.org/~crights/nc2.html

The National Civil Rights Museum, located in Memphis's Lorraine Motel, where Dr. Martin Luther King Jr. was assassinated on April 4, 1968, presents an overview of the long and continuing struggle for civil rights. Exhibits, which include The Freedom Riders and James Meredith's March Against Fear, are arranged in chronological order beginning with the historic *Brown v. Topeka Board of Education* decision.

Negro Leagues Baseball Museum

http://www.blackbaseball.com

J. S. Riley, Director of Research for the Negro Leagues Baseball Museum in Kansas City, Missouri, will help your students examine the historical context of the formation of the League, organized in 1920. He'll introduce your students to players such as Cool Papa Bell, known as the fastest man ever to play the game. Cool Papa was officially clocked circling all of the bases in 12 seconds and was the only player ever to hit a triple on a bunt. This trip will allow your students to examine the historical context of the leagues, why they were formed, and why they no longer exist.

Negro Leagues Baseball Online Archive

http://www.negroleaguebaseball.com

This award-winning tour covers the era of baseball from 1880 to 1955. The impact of segregation comes alive with such stories as the team that waited on tables at a Florida resort at night and played baseball during the day. While reading copies of the historical *Black Ball News*, a journal devoted exclusively to the league, you're likely to run into team members such as Roy Campanella and Willie Mays. The league was so popular that an estimated 40,000 spectators attended the series playoffs in Chicago's Comiskey Park. You may want to steer your students away from the gift shop, which sells posters and other memorabilia.

Nineteenth-Century African American Photographs

http://digital.nypl.org/schomburg/images_aa19

This tour of the digital collection of the Schomburg Center for Research in Black Culture—a national research library that documents the experiences of peoples of African descent throughout the world—presents the work of dozens of artists, engravers, and photographers. The images, categorized by men, women, children, and various topics such as Civil War, Reconstruction, family, labor, and organizations and institutions, document the social, political, and cultural life of the times, from slavery through "quasi-freedom." Key word searches are also available.

Seneca Village

http://projects.ilt.columbia.edu/seneca/start.html

Take your middle school students to early nineteenth-century Seneca Village, New York City's first significant community of African American property holders. Primary source documents, dating from 1925, help students think about life in the community, which was razed in the 1850s to make way for Central Park for the upper classes. This field trip encourages students to use documents such as census entries and affidavits of petition to exercise their critical thinking skills. Essays by sixth and seventh graders provide powerful examples of what can happen when young students respond to primary source materials.

Underground Railroad

http://www.nationalgeographic.com/features/99/railroad

Imagine that you are a slave. You've heard stories about escapes to freedom and can hear the rumblings about the Underground Railroad while you're toiling six days a week in the fields. Although the thought of freedom is compelling, you know that there are extreme risks, and you've heard that the 560-mile-long journey can take as long as a year—assuming you don't get caught. Is it worth it? If you decide to run, the first person you'll encounter is Harriet Tubman (known as Moses), who will show you how to follow the North Star to freedom in Canada. Along the way you'll be faced with many crucial decisions. There is a lot of help along the way, and you'll briefly encounter some of the many white and black *Faces of Freedom,* such as Jermain Loguen (Underground agent and ordained minister who helped 1,500 escapees), Frederick Douglass, Allan Pinkerton (who managed an underground depot before starting his detective agency), and Jonathan Walker (who was imprisoned and branded with an SS for Slave Stealer on his hand for helping seven slaves sail from Florida to the Bahamas). Teachers should check the *Classroom Ideas* section, where lesson plans are classified by grades K–4, 5–8, and 9–12.

AMERICAN REVOLUTION

Liberty Bell

http://www.ushistory.org/libertybell

What weighs over 2,000 pounds and can sound a perfect e-flat tone despite a crack in its 12-foot circumference? Your students can join the 1.5 million annual visitors to Philadelphia's Liberty Bell to find out the answer to such questions as why "Pennsylvania" is misspelled on the bell. The tour includes historical photographic essays, facts, trivia, and quotations, accompanied by the music of John Philip Sousa.

Marching Tour

http://www.ushistory.org/march/index.html

Philadelphia's Independence Hall Association, an historic preservation society, follows the history, battles, and encampments of the American Revolution from 1775 to 1777. Students can follow the war from the landing of the British troops commanded by General Howe at Elks Head, Maryland, to the final moments of the British occupation of Philadelphia to Washington and his troops at Valley Forge, while listening to music of the times. Multimedia games are available to test knowledge gained from the tour.

Valley Forge

http://www.ushistory.org/valleyforge/history/index.html

For six months, Washington and his 12,000 soldiers—some of them as young as 12 years old—camped at Valley Forge, struggling against a harsh winter, low morale, and dwindling provisions. Now, thanks to the Valley Forge Historical Society, your class is able to visit the encampment and share the experiences of soldiers through their journals, letters, and personal effects. Some of the most famous people in American history will also be there. Find out why the Allen brothers may have been partially responsible for Benedict Arnold becoming a traitor, and join the boys and men of the Revolutionary War while they build huts for shelter, play cricket, and put on plays. Students will also be able to meet the field hospital physicians and surgeons, working for daily wages of $4.00 to $6.00, and participate in secret negotiations between Lafayette and Ben Franklin. You may want to read the on-site weather reports from 1775 before you embark on your journey.

Williamsburg, Virginia

http://www.history.org

The Colonial Williamsburg Foundation will take you on a tour of the area where the Revolutionary War was won and introduce you to George and Martha Washington, Patrick Henry, and George Wythe, the gentleman who taught law to Jefferson and James Madison. Students will be able to experience colonial life by spending time with the Geddys in their home and their foundry, where they craft guns, buckles, cutlery, and swords. The Randolphs, an influential family, are also affable hosts. Mr. Randolph presided over Virginia assemblies and chaired the first meeting of delegates from 13 colonies in Philadelphia in 1774. Feel free to wander through Gloucester Street to the Raleigh Tavern, where you are likely to run into Washington or Jefferson. Teachers will want to view the on-site lesson plans.

ANCIENT ATHENS

See also Chapter 2—Greece.
http://www.indiana.edu/~kglowack/athens

The Department of Classical Studies at the University of Indiana at Bloomington has compiled a photo archive of archaeological and architectural remains at ancient Athens. There are dozens of dramatic photographs of landmarks such as the Agora, the Acropolis, and the Arch of Hadrian, arranged by chief excavated regions and monuments. Administrators welcome comments and suggestions (via e-mail) from K–12 teachers and students.

ANCIENT CIVILIZATIONS

http://www.umich.edu/~kelseydb

There is always an interesting ancient tour to take, courtesy of the University of Michigan's Kelsey Museum. If you've missed one, check the archives of past tours such as *Portals to Eternity,* featuring the Necropolis at Terenouthis in lower Egypt; *Preserving Eternity,* a collection of Egyptian funerary artifacts; or tours to ancient Nubia, Byzantium, and ancient Greece or Rome. When we last checked, a tour was about to leave for a trip back to seventh- to fourth-century B.C. ancient Egypt to explore fashion, food, and magic.

ANCIENT EGYPT

Duke Papyrus Archive

http://odyssey.lib.duke.edu/papyrus

Few remnants remain of what was once the most important writing material of the ancient world. The Duke Papyrus Archive is a collection of 1,373 papyri recovered from mummy cartonnage found in a cemetery near the ancient town of Heracleopolis. The texts and images are browsable by subject or key word, and are available in various magnifications. The tour includes an extensive background on papyri and papyrology.

Monument Cyberjourney

http://www.guardians.net/egypt

Panoramic technology allows students to feel as if they are actually walking through such monuments as the pyramids, the Sphinx, the Sun Temple of Niuserre, and the inner chambers of the recently opened Red Pyramid. The hosts provide excellent informative narratives to accompany the visual tour, and Dr. Zahi Hawass, Undersecretary of State for the Giza Monuments, will tell your students about restoration and preservation efforts.

Pyramids

http://www.pbs.org/wgbh/nova/pyramid/

The 1908 edition of *Baedeker's Egypt* cautions that, "Travelers who are in the slightest degree predisposed to apoplectic or fainting fits and ladies traveling alone should not attempt to penetrate into these stifling resources." Despite the warning, you won't want to miss this tour of the ancient pyramids, hosted by the PBS *Nova* series. Be sure to take advantage of the maps provided before you explore the pyramid's mazes. Administrators will tell you about the pharaohs who reside there and provide an excellent background on how the pyramids were constructed. Some may prefer to stay above ground with the archaeologists as they excavate the ancient bakery, built to feed the workers. Mark Lehner, the head of the team, concentrates on the lives of the common people of the era. Teachers should not miss the on-site guide with ideas for using the tour to incorporate archaeology, physics, and engineering into the curriculum.

ANCIENT LIBRARY OF QUMRAN—DEAD SEA SCROLLS

http://metalab.unc.edu/expo/deadsea.scrolls.exhibit/intro.html

Travel back in time to the ancient Dead Sea region with the Library of Congress. Your students will not only be able to see 12 Dead Sea Scroll fragments but also will experience the Qumran community from which the scrolls likely originated. Learn how the scrolls were discovered and the intricacies of scroll research. During the tour, students will also see artifacts on loan from the Israel Antiquities Authority.

ANCIENT MIDDLE EAST

http://www-oi.uchicago.edu/OI/MUS/OI_Museum.html

In the 1930s, the heyday of archaeological expeditions to the Middle East, the University of Chicago's Oriental Institute was among the leading institutions in this field. This tour provides a sample of images from the institute's photographic archives showing now-vanished temples and tombs, famed archaeologists standing by their greatest finds, and digs and artifacts. Students can visit ancient Egypt, Iran, Mesopotamia, Syria, Palestine, Anatolia, Assyria, and Cyprus. Be sure to read the *Mummy's Memo,* in which he complains to the Institute's staff about his hastening deterioration from the current climatic conditions in the Midwest. Students are then able to explore further to learn what efforts are being made to keep the mummy preserved.

ANCIENT OLYMPICS

http://devlab.dartmouth.edu/olympic

In ancient times, athletes competed solely for the honor of being an Olympic victor, not for salaries or endorsements. For over 1,100 years (776 B.C. to A.D. 393), warfare stopped every four years for five days as thousands of people gathered in northwestern Greece to watch the Olympic games. Now your students can also attend, courtesy of the *Ancient Olympic Games Virtual Museum*. Begin in the museum lobby, which allows access to a number of areas such as the *Hall of Definitions* and the *Anecdotes Room*. Dartmouth professors will reveal how cheating was dealt with, what awards were given, and why the original games ended. Be cautioned that females will have to stay within the museum, as the ancient Greek government strictly forbids them to watch the games. The less sports minded may prefer to tour ancient Greece and explore the Temples of Zeus and Hera and other landmarks.

BRITISH HISTORY

See also Chapter 2—England.

Georgian England—Origins of Modern Childhood

http://www.bampfa.berkeley.edu/exhibits/newchild/index.html

This tour puts the current pressures of childhood into perspective by tracing the history of childhood from 1730 to 1830 through Georgian English artwork. Narratives describe the social context of the paintings in nine sections: *The Age of Innocence; The Georgian Family and the Parental Role; Childbirth and Nursery; Child's Play Toys and Recreation; The Child Learns; Children and Charity; Children, Class and Countryside; The Family and Sentiment;* and *When Children Aren't Children.* The self-guided tour, *Young People and Their Families,* asks questions that will spur interesting classroom discussions about childhood and art interpretation. There are also a timeline of eighteenth-century events and an interview with the exhibit's curator.

History Tour

http://britannia.com/history

Historian David Nash Ford has selected tours of some of the most interesting places and events in British history, from prehistoric to modern times. Explore such places as Winchester (the ancient capital of the Anglo-Saxon kingdom of Wessex), ancient Gloucester, and the lands of King Arthur with the help of timelines, narratives, primary source documents, biographies, maps, glossaries, and photographs. While exploring, students can find out why Guy Fawkes Day is celebrated and help solve the mystery of King Arthur's cross.

CANADIAN HISTORY

See also Chapter 2—Canada—Glenbow.

Calgary Aerospace Museum

http://www.asmac.ab.ca

This tour of Calgary's Aerospace Museum documents Canada's aviation and military history. There are over 100 photographs of military planes from World War I on, as well as historic civilian planes, helicopters, and airplane engines, each presented in the context of the history of the aerospace industry and world events. Be sure to check the war heroes to whom this tour is dedicated.

CHICAGO HISTORICAL SOCIETY

http://www.chicagohs.org

It isn't just about Chicago! The Chicago Historical Society is always full of surprises, which change regularly. When we last checked, special exhibits featured a tour of the Michigan Canal, an insight into the diverse worlds of George Washington and Sally Rand (*What George Wore and Sally Didn't*), a trip to the Wild West, and a visit to the Civil War Reconstruction era. The Society uses the Internet in creative ways. For example, the Chicago Fire exhibit includes stereographic three-dimensional images of Chicago in ashes.

CIVIL WAR

See also African American History, Museums—The Lincoln Museum, Chapter 9—Galleries and Museums—National Museum of American Art, and Chapter 13—Davis, Jefferson; Meade, George; and Thomas, George Henry.

Battle of Chickamauga

http://www.19thalabama.org/battles/chickamauga/index.html

Travel back to September 1863 and relive the 10-day Battle of Chickamauga from the perspective of infantrymen. Join former farmers, shopkeepers, and other citizens as they battle for Chattanooga, a key rail center and gateway to Confederate territory. Texts are accompanied by photographs, so you can get a good sense of how topography influenced strategies and outcomes.

Battle of Gettysburg

http://www.nps.gov/gett/home.htm

Revisit the Battle of Gettysburg, courtesy of the United States National Park Service. Students will be able to experience life as an infantryman and discover the similarities between the troops of the Army of the Potomac, commanded by Major General George G. Meade, and the Army of Northern Virginia, under General Robert E. Lee. Members of both troops were surprised at how long the battle lasted, and both had similar drills and weapons. Experience military life in the 1860s as you learn what to wear and how to pitch a dog tent and try to acquire a taste for hardtack, worm castles, and skillygalee. The Service has a special tour for those who want to learn how to become "junior historians."

Battle of Mobile Bay

http://www.maf.mobile.al.us/recreation/area_history/battle.html

The Battle of Mobile Bay is known as the "beginning of the end for the Confederacy" and the first battle in which new technological developments of modern warfare such as iron ships, rifled guns, explosive shells, and mines were used. The trip begins during the early morning hours of August 5, 1864, as the federal fleet begins its attack on Fort Morgan. Watch as wooden ships are lashed together in pairs, led by the *Tecumseh* and other ironclad ships. Although the *Tecumseh* will be lost when it hits a mine, the battle will be the first major success of General Ulysses S. Grant's strategy to re-elect Lincoln in 1864 and end the Civil War by military victory rather than negotiated peace.

Civil War Center

http://www.cwc.lsu.edu

Take your class to the United States Civil War Center at Louisiana State University. The hosts will share over 18,000 documents and photographs with your students, including the government's standing orders for the Union Army, the official state of Massachusetts casualty list, lists of Jewish American soldiers, emancipation proclamations of various states, the personal papers of Jefferson Davis, and pictures of and texts on Confederate symbols.

Civil War Women

http://odyssey.lib.duke.edu/collections/civil-war-women.html

Duke University's *Civil War Women* exhibit brings students face to face with women such as Rose O'Neal Greenhow, one of the most renowned spies of the Civil War. Rose was so successful at her occupation that Jefferson Davis credited the victorious Battle of Manassas to her efforts. In contrast, read the diary of 16-year-old Alice Williamson, which chronicles the occupation of Gallatin and the surrounding region by Union forces.

Fort Sumter

http://www.tulane.edu/~latner/CrisisMain.html

It is Monday, March 4, 1861. You are Abraham Lincoln and have just been elected to the presidency. All efforts to achieve compromise between the North and South have failed, and issues such as secession and ownership of federal property loom before you. Although you strongly oppose secession, you must consider public opinion, the Constitution, and other factors. There is still time to change your Inaugural Address before you state your policies before the nation. This interactive decision-making simulation, developed by Richard Latner of Tulane University, uses text, images, and sound to place students in the role of Abraham Lincoln during the period of time between his election to the presidency and the Battle of Fort Sumter. Presented with the facts, students must choose a course of action at five critical junctures. It's a tremendous responsibility because the entire course of history will be affected. However, advice is available from advisors, newspapers, friends, and political figures. Although the site allows students to view the decisions actually made by Lincoln, Latner suggests that the experience will be more useful if students first make their own decisions. There are an online notebook to record your thoughts, historical commentaries, primary source documents, and "hot words" that link to additional information.

Galutia York

http://www.snymor.edu/pages/library/local_history/civil_war

Galutia York was a 19-year-old from Hubbardsville, New York, who responded to President Lincoln's request for volunteers to fight in the Civil War. Less than one year later, after seeing several battles, he died of an illness. Colgate University has collected letters written by York, as well as maps and photographs, including the hospital at Fort Monroe, Virginia, where he died.

Library of Congress Photographs

http://rs6.loc.gov/cwphome.html

The Civil War was the first war to be photographed. Pay a visit to the Library of Congress, where over 1,100 of these images, most of which were taken under the supervision of Matthew Brady, are on display. Photographs are searchable by key word or subject matter, including military personnel and battlefield scenes.

Music and Poetry

http://www.erols.com/kfraser

General Robert E. Lee insisted, "There would have been no army without music." This tour provides song lyrics and poetry written by soldiers rather than professional or polished poets, and as such, conveys the inner thoughts and emotions of actual participants. The materials are divided into authors, titles, and first lines, as well as Confederate and Union works, which are further categorized by battles, officers, a soldier's life, post war reminiscences, etc. The administrator has added author biographical information, when available.

Virginia Military Institute Archives
http://www.vmi.edu/~archtml/index.html

Civil War resources available at this Virginia Military Institute (VMI) tour include photographs, diaries, official records, biographical materials, and manuscripts dating from the founding of the school in 1839. There are extensive materials on General Thomas J. (Stonewall) Jackson, a VMI faculty member who taught natural and experimental philosophy and instruction of artillery. We learned that Jackson did not have "the qualifications needed for so important a chair. He was no teacher and he lacked the tact required in getting along with his classes." There are also biographical sketches of the many Civil War generals who attended VMI, as well as materials related to the Patton family and the Battle of New Market.

GERMAN HISTORICAL MUSEUM
http://www.dhm.de

True historical studies should encompass the viewpoints and perspectives of many nations and cultures. A visit to Berlin's German Historical Museum, with tours available in several languages, will allow students to gain an understanding of history from the German viewpoint. Past exhibitions, archived on site, include artifacts and historical documents from the ninth century to the present; past relationships and encounters between Germany and the countries of Denmark, Norway, and Sweden; a multimedia exhibit about the Socialist Unity Party; photographs of post-World War II Germany; and the 1989 demonstrations in East Berlin. This is an excellent tour for history and German language students.

GULF WAR
http://www.pbs.org/wgbh/pages/frontline/gulf/

Thanks to the PBS *Frontline* series, your students can watch the Gulf War all over again. In addition to maps and vivid photographs, an interview with Major Rhonda Cornum, whose helicopter was shot down during a search and rescue mission, will challenge your students' gender expectations. With broken arms and other injuries, she was captured by the Iraqis. Her story begins (you can either read or hear it) when the Iraqis discover that she is female. Other sections of the tour include weapons and technology, interviews with the politicians and military decision makers, analyses by two journalists, and an interview with Iraqi Foreign Minister Tariq Assiz.

HOLOCAUST
http://remember.org

The *Holocaust Cybrary*, an immense site, attempts to make the horrors of the Holocaust real and immediate through stories, experiences, and dynamic discussions. Administrator Mike Dunn is especially interested in promoting discussions with high school students. Unlike other Holocaust sites, the *Cybrary* de-emphasizes more famous authors and focuses on poems, articles, and book excerpts from survivors and their relatives. Also included are a complete curriculum and teacher's guide.

INTERNATIONAL HORSE MUSEUM
http://www.imh.org

Although the first horses were no larger than a fox, they and their descendants became an integral part of world history. The International Horse Museum presents an interesting historical tour organized by the various roles played by the horse. The tour begins in 56 B.C. and covers such notables and eras as Attila the Hun, the early draft horse in America, and soldiers' horses on the Western frontier.

LIBRARY OF CONGRESS
http://lcweb.loc.gov

Think of having the United States Library of Congress, with all of its primary source documents, audio files, and videotapes, across the street from your school. Exhibits at the online facility frequently change, and even the many permanent online exhibits are always adding material, so we suggest that any time your class is studying American history, literature, science, or social studies, you pay a visit to the facility. To give you an idea of the breadth of materials available to your classroom, consider the huge *American Memory* permanent exhibit with its hundreds of primary source materials, including original documents from the Continental Congress, manuscripts and photographs from folklore interviews of the WPA Writers' Project, and Walt Whitman's notebooks. Students are able to hear voices from all walks of life in U.S. history—from a mill worker in North Carolina to great authors and politicians.

MAYANS

Journey Through Tikal
http://www.destination360.com/tikal/guide.htm

Did you ever wonder what a 2,000-year-old skyscraper would look like? Take a trip back in time to the ancient Mayan city of Tikal, to its temples and treasures. Maps are provided; simply click on the places you

would like to explore. The hosts provide movies and 360-degree panoramic views. Temple IV, built in A.D. 741, is 212 feet high—a precursor to
the modern skyscraper. Students will learn how the ancient Mayans were
able to accurately predict solstices and knew the length of an average year
on both Earth and Venus. If you have time, stop in at the ball court. The
game is similar to soccer, but the consequences of defeat are much more
severe.

Tour 1

http://www.halfmoon.org

It's rare that one gets to visit with a common Mayan because most
tours cover the ruling class and their monuments and temples. Although
those usual sites are available on this tour, there is a great deal of concen-
tration on daily life. The Mayans will show you how to make your own
Mayan calendar, write your name in hieroglyphics, and play Mayan
games. Don't worry about the language—there's an online translation
program. Before you embark on your journey, you might want to learn
how to be attractive to other Mayans by shaping your head, arranging
your eyes, and decorating your teeth. Teachers should be aware that administrators of this site are selling t-shirts, magnets, and other items, and
that there is a link to the Lizzie Borden House, so supervision may be
advisable.

 # MUSEUMS

See also Chapter 2—Japan—Tokugawa Art Museum.

Illinois State Museum

http://www.museum.state.il.us/exhibits/index.html

The Illinois State Museum in Springfield uses the Internet in novel
ways to make history come alive. You won't be able to see everything in
one day, but feel free to stop by as often as you like to see the permanent
and temporary exhibits. Be sure not to miss *At Home in the Heartland*,
which covers Illinois family life from 1700 to the present. Students
choose answers that determine how a particular story will unfold, and
along the way, they'll learn much more than mere facts about the time and
place they're studying. They actually become a part of the story and begin
to pay attention to details of place, customs, and decor. For example, as
Nicholas Chassin, a royal storekeeper, they must decide how to finish
completing their home by procuring a certain "article of furniture"—an
interesting classroom discussion is certain to result when they find that
Nicholas is actually talking about a wife. The museum also has teacher resources for grades 3–5, 6–9, and 10–12 that cover language arts, art and
geography, and social studies, as well as games and puzzles. Natural history tours include *Mazon Creek Fossils*, which shows fossils recovered
from the Francis Creek Shale, and an extensive tour of the *Midwestern
United States 16,000 Years Ago*.

The Lincoln Museum

http://www.thelincolnmuseum.org/museum_index.html

A tour of the Lincoln Museum offers a comprehensive view of the life and legacy of Abraham Lincoln and of the United States during his lifetime. There are several multimedia galleries, including *Lincoln's America*, *Prairie Politician to President*, *Civil War*, *Ford Theater*, and *Family Album*. Teachers should not miss the *Guide to the Emancipation Proclamation*, with lesson plans and other materials.

Museum of Antiquities

http://www.ncl.ac.uk/~nantiq

Take your students to the largest museum of archaeology in northeast England, a joint venture of the Society of Antiquaries of Newcastle upon Tyne and the University of Newcastle upon Tyne. Tours of the region include Hadrian's Wall and the Roman frontier. Stop and visit exhibits reflecting life in the region from early prehistory through the seventeenth century, and be sure to catch *Flints and Stones*, with separate sections for adults and students. Students can spend time with the Shaman and an archaeologist while traveling back in time. After the tour, there is a food quiz designed to see if they could survive as hunters and gatherers today by picking the right foods. There is also a teacher's guide, readily adaptable to classes in any country. For example, using cardboard tubes and marbles, students construct their own water system, modeled after the Roman system.

OREGON TRAIL

http://home.4w.com/pages/hoppe/journal/intro.htm

John McTurk Gibson and his companion, John W. Powell, traveled the Oregon-California trails during the Pikes Peak gold rush. Gibson's great-great grandson (also named John McTurk Gibson) shares the journals the two kept from the time they began the trek from their home in Marengo, Iowa. Clickable maps of Nebraska, Wyoming, Utah, California, and Nevada allow students to go directly to various destinations along the trail. There is also an extensive index classified by supplies, names of people and places, and topics.

PALEOLITHIC PAINTED CAVE

http://www.culture.fr/culture/arcnat/chauvet/en/gvpda-d.htm

Experience historical spelunking in this vast network of underground caves and Paleolithic artwork recently discovered in the south of France. The caves, dating from the Paleolithic age, allow students to study ancient cultures. Your hosts are the Minister of Culture and the Biblioteque Universalis, and tours are available in both English and French.

PIRATES

Tour 1

http://www.nationalgeographic.com/pirates/maina.html

Thanks to the folks at *National Geographic,* your students can sail the seven seas aboard a pirate ship, choosing their own pirate name and three different adventures. All the famous pirates will be there, including the Barbarossa brothers, who plagued the Mediterranean Seas for years; Edward Teach, better known as Blackbeard; Henry Morgan, who later was knighted in England; and Ching Shih, a woman who commanded nearly 8,000 coed pirates. Females in your class will revel at the story of Mary Read and Anne Bonny, who bravely fought against the British Royal Navy in 1720 while the male pirates "cowered in drunkenly fear." Administrators want you to note that the pirates on this trip are real, and each adventure draws facts from history. However, details are their own creation.

Tour 2

http://despina.advanced.org/16438/index.shtml

This tour is more textually based than tour 1, but has more factual information such as a history of piracy dating back to 1350 B.C. In addition to meeting such pirates as Jean Laffitte of New Orleans and Sir Francis Drake, your class can learn the difference between pirates, buccaneers, Corsairs, and privateers while experiencing life at sea. Whether you choose to take the guided tour or wander the seven seas alone, there's a lot to learn. For example, despite their reputation for harsh democracy, pirate society was the first to introduce workmen's compensation.

SOVIET UNION

http://metalab.unc.edu/pjones/russian/outline.html

The Library of Congress will take your students on a tour covering the first public display of highly secret internal records of Soviet Communist rule. After the Soviet archivist explains how and why primary source documents such as letters from Gorky to Stalin were accumulated, students can then learn about the internal workings of the Soviet Union from 1917 on. They'll gain a new appreciation of freedom as they learn about the secret police, collectivization, the deportation of Tatars following World War II, and the problems of the intelligentsia and dissidents such as Boris Pasternak. One of the more fascinating documents we found was the results of internal investigation of the nuclear incident at Chernobyl.

SPANISH-AMERICAN WAR

http://www.spanam.simplenet.com

Take a trip back in time to the Spanish-American War. One of the major benefits of this tour is its well-rounded representation of primary source documents from both sides of the war and from all walks of life. There are first-hand accounts from troops stationed in Cuba, Guam, Hawaii, the American home front, the Philippines, and Puerto Rico; and Theodore Roosevelt's accounts of the Battles of San Juan and Kettle Hills. Students can tour the ships of the U.S. and Spanish navies and view profiles, medals, uniforms, and photos of fighting troops, journalists, etc. Don't miss the virtual tour of the USS *Olympia*, Admiral Dewey's flagship at the Battle of Manila Bay.

TITANIC

http://www.fireflyproductions.com/titanic

Get ready to board the *Titanic*. Leonardo Dicaprio will not be aboard, but the actual crew members will introduce you to the other passengers and allow you to explore the ill-fated ship from the boat deck down to the boiler room. The tour is filled with facts and trivia, as well as information about the lives of the survivors after the tragedy, details that make one realize the enormity of the incident.

UNITED STATES—ADRIAN SCOTT AND THE HOLLYWOOD TEN

See also Chapter 13—McCarthy, Joseph.

http://www.otal.umd.edu/~rccs/blacklist

Imagine having to choose between working as a successful writer, actor, or producer or as a short-order cook. This was one of the choices faced by the "Hollywood Ten" and other "blacklistees" during the years of investigations by the House of Representative's Committee on Un-American Activities. Centered around Adrian Scott, a playwright, screenwriter, and producer, this tour takes students through the accusations of Communist infiltration into the motion picture industry. Through primary source documents and other materials, students will gain an understanding of the difficult choices faced by those in the industry. The tour can spur interesting classroom discussions as students are faced with the choices of admitting unwarranted guilt and providing the committee with other names to investigate, continuing to work under pseudonyms, seeking alternative employment, or leaving the country.

UNITED STATES—CONSTITUTION
http://www.nara.gov/education/teaching/constitution/home.html

The National Archives and Records Administration (NARA) has established a series of sites that allow the implementation of United States National History Standards and National Standards for History and Government into the curriculum through primary source documents. Students are able to travel back in time to Independence Hall and meet the 39 delegates who signed the Constitution on September 17, 1787. Teachers will want to check the lesson plans and activities and find out, for example, how to prepare a classroom simulation that allows students to experience how the delegates may have felt while gathering for the first time to write the Constitution.

UNITED STATES—NATIONAL ARCHIVES AND RECORDS ADMINISTRATION
http://www.nara.gov/exhall/exhibits.html

The National Archives and Records Administration (NARA) in Washington, D.C., maintains a number of exhibits relating to American history. *Tokens and Treasures* is an exhibit of gifts given to 12 U.S. presidents by citizens and various heads of states. The *American Originals* exhibit allows students to view some of NARA's most interesting and famous documents, including the Louisiana Purchase, a police report on the Lincoln assassination, Nixon's letter of resignation, FDR's declaration of war, and the verdict against Al Capone. Other exhibits include an original copy of the Constitution (including the rarely seen second page); poster art from World War II; the photographs of Pulitzer Prize winner John H. White (*Portraits of Black Chicago*); the behind-the-scenes story of Elvis Presley's 1970 visit with Richard Nixon in the Oval Office; and art, documents, and photographs produced by Works Project Administration employees during the New Deal.

UNITED STATES—NEW DEAL ERA
http://newdeal.feri.org/feri/ndn.htm

The New Deal Network, an organization devoted to examining the programs and policies of Franklin Delano Roosevelt, provides over 20,000 photographs, biographies, political cartoons, audio clips, and primary source documents from the New Deal period. There are also curricular materials and rotating features that cover specific topics such as the Tennessee Valley Authority and the Depression in further detail. All items in the tour, which vary from public health posters created by the Works Project Administration (WPA) to court testimony, are searchable by author, year, and topic. Administrators invite students to document WPA and similar projects in their own communities and to report their findings to the New Deal Network. The tour is geared toward middle and high school students.

UNITED STATES—1918–1921
http://newman.baruch.cuny.edu/digital/redscare

Through primary source documents, including photographs, advertisements, and political cartoons, students are able to travel back to the United States during the period following World War I through the mid-1920s. The tour is presented through the lens of the Red Scare, the fear of Communism that followed Russia's Bolshevik Revolution. Materials portray the tremendous fears and uncertainties of the times caused by epidemics, strikes, hyper-inflation, race riots, and espionage scares, as well as responses ranging from sedition laws to Prohibition. The hundreds of photographs, advertisements, and political cartoons from the digital collections at Newman Library, Baruch College, at CUNY are filed chronologically and by subject headings.

UNITED STATES—1950s
http://www.joesherlock.com/fifties.html

Joe Sherlock, a 1950s aficionado, tells us that the 1950s were not just a decade, but a state of mind. It was the era of stay-at-home moms, stylish cars, full-service gasoline stations, Elvis, and safety. Pay a visit to Joe's site as he reviews the era through memorable events, photographs, and music. He tells us that "over 50,504 tubes of Duco cement were used to glue the molded polystyrene pink and charcoal plastic tiles to his site."

UNITED STATES—1950s ROAD TRIP
http://www2.kenyon.edu/people/slomanj/main.htm

The 1950s era was the beginning of the end of the old U.S. highways, with their billboards, service stations, motels, and roadside diners. Hop in the rag top car with your students, turn on the radio, and revisit the era, traveling down the Dixie Highway stretching from Ontario, Canada, to Miami, Florida. It's worth the trip just to read the old Burma Shave signs: "Use this cream/a day or two/then don't call her /she'll call you." Students will be amazed when they hear about sign ideas that were rejected because they were considered offensive, such as "My man won't shave/said Hazel Huz/But I don't worry/Dora's does."

UNITED STATES—1968
http://www.stg.brown.edu/projects/1968/

The Whole World Was Watching is an oral history project jointly developed by Rhode Island's South Kingstown High School and Brown University's Scholarly Technology Group. The project relates and analyzes events that occurred during 1968 through transcripts, audio recordings, and interviews conducted by high school sophomores during the spring of 1998. Rhode Island citizens from all walks of life discuss the Vietnam War, the struggle for civil rights, women's issues, and the assassinations of Martin Luther King Jr. and Robert Kennedy. Kathy Spoehr talks about her transition from a conservative upbringing in a wealthy suburb of Chicago to political activism at Brown University, while another citizen relates her inability to obtain credit without her husband's signature. The tour, geared toward high school students, includes a glossary, timeline, and bibliography.

UNITED STATES—NINETEENTH CENTURY
http://www.nps.gov/jeff

Pay a visit to St. Louis, Missouri's Museum of Westward Expansion, courtesy of the United States National Park Service. Nineteenth-century Native Americans, pioneers, mountain men and trappers, soldiers, farmers, buffalo hunters, miners, and cowboys share their stories as they shape the history of the United States. Those with real audio players can listen to Thomas Jefferson speak of his many accomplishments, William Clark talking about his expedition to the Pacific Ocean, a buffalo soldier sharing his struggles after the Civil War, and an overland woman's adventures as she heads west.

UNITED STATES—WOMEN'S LIBERATION MOVEMENT
See also United States—1968.

http://odyssey.lib.duke.edu/wlm

Professor Anne Valk of Duke University provides this collection of documents focusing on the U.S. women's liberation movement from the late 1960s to the early 1970s. The wide-ranging tour includes radical theory, humorous plays, and the minutes of meetings of various grassroots groups. The documents are searchable by topics including medical and reproductive rights, music, organizations, women of color, and women's work rights and roles. Teachers should be advised that the collection is all-inclusive and includes areas on sexuality and lesbian feminism.

A WALK THROUGH TIME
http://physics.nist.gov/GenInt/Time/time.html

This tour covers the evolution of time measurement, from ancient calendars through the earliest clocks to the *Atomic Age of Time Standards*. Students will be in safe hands with the National Institute of Standards and Technology, an agency of the Technology Administration of the Department of Commerce.

WORLD WAR I

http://memory.loc.gov/ammem/nfhome.html

The Library of Congress has an extensive collection of World War I documents, images, and audio recordings. Students can follow the events leading to the war, and along the way they are certain to encounter such notables as General John Pershing, James Watson Gerard, and Samuel Gompers. There is also a multimedia exhibit covering the presidential election of 1920 (Warren G. Harding and Calvin Coolidge on the Republican ticket and James Cox and Franklin Delano Roosevelt on the Democratic ticket).

WORLD WAR II

See also A-Bomb Museum, African American Newspaper Company's History Museum, United States—National Archives and Records Administration, and Chapter 13—Murphy, Audie, and Truman, Harry.

Battle of the Atlantic

http://www.mariner.org/atlantic/index.htm

The Mariners Museum in Newport News, Virginia, brings your students to the Battle of the Atlantic, where U-boats, submarine hunters, battleships, and destroyers hunt one another mercilessly. It's a story of valor, naval intelligence, strategy, and death, told through photographs and videos and sound. The historic footage includes the capture of the German U-505 submarine.

Female Journalists, Photographers and Broadcasters

http://lcweb.loc.gov/exhibits/wcf/wcf0001.html

World War II marked the first major foray of women into the workforce and offered one of the first professional opportunities for female journalists. This Library of Congress exhibit spotlights eight women who succeeded in going to the front during the war: Therese Bonney, Toni Frissell, Marvin Breckenridge Patterson, Clare Booth Luce, Janet Flanner, Esther Bubley, Dorothea Lange, and May Craig.

National Archives and Records Administration Exhibit Hall

http://www.nara.gov/exhall/people/people.html

The United States federal government's National Archives and Records Administration (NARA) exhibit, *People of War*, highlights the contributions of thousands of American civilians and military personnel who served during World War II, preceded by a detailed background on events leading up to the war. Students will be able to spend some time with people from all walks of life, from the brothers whose deaths led to the passage of the Sullivan Law to Joseph Kennedy. The visit brings the social climate of the times into sharp focus as students spend time with some of the special units formed to accommodate minorities, such as the Code Talkers, a unit of Navajo Indians who used their native language for radio transmissions. The Japanese were never able to decipher their "coded" transmissions. The role that scientists played in the development of the DUKW (the amphibious trucks that we call ducks) and the development of the M-1 Garand rifle is also examined. Stick around until the end of the war to sit in on the meeting of American and Russian troops at the Elbe and attend the surrender ceremony.

CHAPTER 2

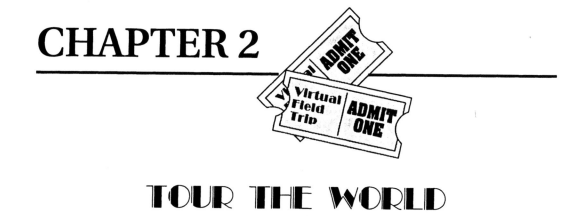

TOUR THE WORLD

Travel the world from pole to pole, from Afghanistan to Wales, without worrying about vaccinations, passports, language problems, or jet lag. Imagine wandering through Antarctica at the same time you're complaining about the malfunctioning classroom air conditioning.

AFGHANISTAN

http://www.afghan-web.com

The people of Afghanistan, known for their generosity and hospitality, welcome your class to the heart of south central Asia. Before you leave, be sure to convert your dollars into Afgani (the current exchange rate is available on site), learn a few phrases in the local languages, and familiarize yourselves with the current customs and politics. Feel free to stop in at the local museums, or spend some time with the locals, who will share recipes, poetry, local wisdom and stories, music, and riddles. The more adventuresome may want to join in a game of Buzkashi (literally translated as "goat grabbing"), the national sport, while others may just want to sit back and watch movies or browse through photographs.

AFRICA

See also Chapter 9—Galleries and Museums—Akan and Yoruba Art and Chapter 13—Mandela, Nelson.

National Parks

http://library.thinkquest.org/16645

Three teenage students from India, the Netherlands, and the United States will take your students on a virtual safari through Africa's national parks, accompanied by sound clips of roaring animals and African chanting and music. When you're tired of hacking through the jungles or trekking across the desert, you may wish to tour the major cities or stop in at an elementary and high school in Cameroon to find out what a typical student's day is like. The *Living Africa* tour is so packed with surprises and treats that we can't cover it all for you—you'll have to go there yourself. For example, you can learn some Swahili language, view a photographic essay of a Gambian family, learn about different religions and ethnic groups, or roll around in the mud with warthogs.

Ghana

http://www.ghanaweb.com/GhanaHomePage/ghana.php3

Francis Akoto, a native Ghanian and design engineer for Noki Telecommunications, invites your students to Ghana. Before beginning the journey, we suggest students study the on-site materials with directions to Ghana and warnings and advice on travel within the country. Learning about the local currency and current events will enable them to make wise consumer decisions and give them things to discuss with the people they'll be meeting. Once in Ghana, they can view the local sites, attend sporting events, and sample the local cuisine. There is even a copy of *Ghana's Top 10 Music Chart,* with a link to Ghana hip-hop music. Among Akoto's numerous other links is the Miss Ghana home page. We strongly suggest that you monitor the *Gossip* and *True Stories* sections ahead of time.

ANDES

See also Chapter 5—Amazon River Dolphins.

http://www.andes.org

Ada and Russ Gibbons share their knowledge of the Andes Mountains and its people on this cultural tour encompassing Peru, Bolivia, Argentina, Ecuador, Chile, and Colombia. We suggest you look over the basic Quechua language lessons before you leave, although many of the people you'll meet during the tour will speak English. There are photographs, songs, movie clips of dances, riddles, short stories, and more. Teachers might want to steer the younger students away from the jokes section.

ANTARCTICA

Tour 1

http://astro.uchicago.edu/cara/vtour

Get ready for a grueling trip to the Center for Astrophysical Research in Antarctica. All travelers must first stop in New Zealand, where they'll be equipped with proper clothing and given a brief lesson in subzero temperature survival. You'll then board specially built U.S. government planes for the eight-hour ride to McMurdo Station, Antarctica's largest community. Scientists will be waiting to take you on a tour of their research station, where they'll carefully explain how specialized equipment is used to study cosmic microwaves, climate, and other scientific principles. A tour of the United States Coast Guard's specially equipped *Polar Star* ship is also available. Or, if you're up for another four-hour flight, travel farther, to the South Pole.

Tour 2

http://www.glacier.rice.edu/

Students from Rice University will be your guides to the geographic features, flora, and fauna of Antarctica. You probably won't be able to see everything on your first trip: The continent is 30 percent larger than the entire United States, and subzero temperatures and 185-mile-per-hour winds will probably slow your travel. Students will learn how Antarctica controls worldwide climate and weather; how penguins, seals, moss, lichen, bacteria, and algae survive; and how scientific experiments are conducted. Teachers can learn how to become part of an actual rather than a virtual team visit sponsored by Rice.

AUSTRALIA

See also Chapter 4—Bird Watching—Birding Southern Queensland and Parks and Sanctuaries—Australian Botanic Gardens and Chapter 6—Australian Animals and Australian Wildlife.

Australian Schools

http://www.herbertonss.qld.edu.au/index.html

Take your students "down under" to far northern Queensland and spend some time with the students at the primary–grade 10 Herberton School. There's always an interesting Australian tour being conducted, from the bushlands to the rainforests. We've had the opportunity to get to know the aboriginal and Torres Strait Islander peoples, spend time at the Kakudu National Park and the Great Barrier Reef, and hang around with Lionel Rose, the Australian boxer.

Primary Grade Activities   PG

http://www.ozemail.com.au/~wprimary/acts.htm

Even your youngest students can travel to Australia, where they'll love hearing the laugh of a kookaburra, coloring a rainbow lorikeet, making a climbing koala or hopping kangaroo, or flying a sugar glider kite.

Tasmania

http://www.parks.tas.gov.au/tpws.html

The Australian Parks and Wildlife Service is eager to share the wonders of Tasmania with students of all ages. Be sure to study the *Bushwalking Guide* before you take any of the walking tours; you'll learn basic survival skills and the safest times of the year to travel. The less physically fit can just sit back and watch slide shows and movies about Tasmania's animal and plant life, much of which is found nowhere else on Earth. There really is a Tasmanian devil (the world's largest surviving carnivorous marsupial), and you can listen to its sounds and watch its ill-tempered performance. Tours of historic sites, including a nineteenth-century coal mine, shipwrecks, and the Ross Female Factory, a former women's prison, are also available.

BOSNIA

Tour 1

http://monarch.gsu.edu/crampton/bosnia

This virtual tour, organized by Jeremy Crampton and Beth Rundstrom of the Department of Geography at Virginia's George Mason University, begins by taking you back in history to the origins of the Bosnian conflict. The tour then continues through time to the Dayton Peace Accords, with each section containing questions that test and stretch student understanding. At the end of the tour, students are requested to choose a role, such as a refugee from Zepa, and answer questions from the chosen perspective.

Tour 2

http://www.snc.edu/leadstud/bosnia-children/

This rather graphic site may upset many of your students because it shows the Bosnian conflict as seen through the eyes of local children. A 10-year-old writes, "My friend is dead. My cousin is dead. I'm scared when I see the dead men on the street. I want this war to stop. And to be peace in all the world." Children relate their actual experiences, through photographs, artwork, letters, and stories gathered by Drs. Stephen Kaplan and Garth Katner of St. Norbert College during a trip to Tuzla during 1996, sponsored by the University of Tuzla and a non-governmental organization affiliated with the University of Amsterdam.

CAMBODIA

See THAILAND

CANADA

See also Chapter 7—Science—Museums and Laboratories—Royal British Columbia Museum.

Canadian Arctic—Leo Ussak School   PG

http://www.arctic.ca/lus

There have been some changes for the kids of Leo Ussak school since *Virtual Field Trips*. They now proudly reside within the new Canadian territory of Nunavut, created on April 1, 1999, and they're eager to share information about their local community and life in the Canadian Arctic. In many ways, they're not much different from kids anywhere else: They spend their summers swimming and playing baseball and love to "jump in mud puddles" in the spring. On the other hand, their favorite foods are caribou and polar bear. Let the students teach you the Inuktitut language; tell you all about Rankin Inlet and Leo Ussak (an Inuit elder); and share northern tales, art, and student multimedia projects. Hopefully, you'll get there in time to take part in the "Time Capsule 2000" project!

Glenbow

http://www.glenbow.org

Glenbow is Canada's foremost center of history and art, housing a museum of western heritage, international cultural collections, an art gallery, a library, and archives of western Canadian history. The art gallery has a collection of historical and modern art, including works by the Inuit people. There are a variety of tours to take, including pictographic robes of the Plains First Indians; sacred objects from the Buddhist and Hindu cultures of Asia; historic glass lantern slides; and an extensive collection covering Canadian cultural history, ethnology, and military history.

National Atlas of Canada

http://atlas.gc.ca/

Students can learn about the geography of Canada through dozens of topographic, demographic, historical, environmental, and other thematic maps. An interactive mapping tool enables students to construct their own maps based on statistics and other data provided during this tour. Selection of various mapping parameters allows students to examine Canadian issues such as aging population, language, natural hazards, and wildlife. There are also an interactive geography quiz, a digital atlas of Canadian communities that allows students to share their perceptions of the communities in which they live, geographical facts, and teaching resources.

CHINA

See also Chapter 9—Arts and Crafts Classes—Chinese Calligraphy and Galleries and Museums—National Palace Museum of Taiwan.

Tour 1

http://pasture.ecn.purdue.edu/~agenhtml/agenmc/china/china.html

Students of Purdue University will take you on a guided cultural tour of China, including the Forbidden City, the Great Wall, and the Imperial Garden. We suggest you check the *Audio Tutorial of Survival Chinese* before you leave, where you'll learn how to say "hello" and how to politely respond to an introduction. Don't forget to sample the food during your tour. An illustrated cookbook will let you share recipes with your friends after you arrive back home.

Tour 2

http://www.chinapage.com/china.html

Professor Emeritus Ming L. Pei hosts this cultural tour covering Chinese classics and arts through 5,000 years of history. Those able to read the Chinese language will find more extensive materials in the *Chinese Reading Room*, while others will want to visit the *China Room*. Pei explains that he's created this Web site entirely on his own, without the support of the university; so much Chinese culture has been lost or destroyed, he says, that he wants to preserve as much as he can and to encourage others to do the same. His selections include readings of poems in both Chinese and English; synopses of short stories, novels, plays, and operas; calligraphy; and information on festivals. He also includes the true story of Mulan and invites students to compare it with the Disney version.

ENGLAND

See also Chapter 1—British History—History Tour and Chapter 13—Prince of Wales.

British Monarchy

http://www.royal.gov.uk

This is the official site of the British monarchy. In addition to biographies of Queen Elizabeth, Prince Charles, and other family members, there is a tribute to Princess Diana and tours of royal palaces and private estates. Parts of the royal collection of art, books, furniture, and jewels (including the famous crown jewels) are also on display. Some of the most interesting portions of the tour are the sections explaining the rules of accession, coronation, and succession, as well as answers to frequently asked questions, where one is able to find out, for example, exactly what "swan upping" is.

No. 10 Downing Street

http://www.number-10.gov.uk/

Number 10 Downing Street has been the official residence of England's prime ministers for over two centuries. Students will be surprised at what lies behind the plain black brick façade of this structure. It's actually constructed of yellow brick, which, in keeping with tradition, has been painted to mirror the appearance of the smog that covered the building until England instituted its Clean Air Act. After students enter one of the two identical front doors, they'll be free to roam the building and its gardens. While wandering through such places as the cabinet room, where Winston Churchill announced the end of World War II, and the "haunted" dining room, students will learn how the British government operates and be able to participate in live broadcasts and discussions. There are also biographies of the current and past prime ministers and a database of speeches and announcements.

Parliament

http://www.explore.parliament.uk

The members of the British Parliament invite your students to participate in an online debating chamber, where they can follow the progress of current legislation and debate the pros and cons of various issues in each step of the legislative process. During the course of debates involving issues such as bans on smoking, students follow the legislative process from initial white papers to first and second readings through the committee and report stages. There is a special section for teachers explaining how to integrate this tour into various curricula. There are interactive puzzles and quizzes with an online search function to help students find the answers. Government officials are available to answer questions via e-mail, but they ask that you first check the online database to see if your questions have already been answered. (We found out, for example, why the queen cannot enter the House of Commons.) A special tour is available for students under the age of 12.

 FRANCE

Le Cordon Bleu Cooking School

http://metalab.unc.edu/expo/restaurant/restaurant.html

Paris's world-famous Le Cordon Bleu cooking school and renowned chefs such as Andre L. Cointreau will be more than happy to teach your students the fundamentals and philosophy of French cuisine. Although the recipes are for haute cuisine and require sophisticated cooking techniques, everything is clearly explained. While you're there you can learn the history of Le Cordon Bleu, which dates back to 1896.

Paris

http://www.paris.org

Stroll through Paris on your own or with a guide (either English or French speaking) while visiting the City of Light's famous landmarks, such as the Louvre, the Champs-Elysees, the Arc de Triomphe, and the Eiffel Tower. Be sure to experience the city's nightlife at the Moulin Rouge, view Paris from the sky, and take a boat ride along the Seine River.

GERMANY

See also Chapter 1—German Historical Museum.

Berlin

http://userpage.chemie.fu-berlin.de/adressen/berlin.html

Students can take a tour guided in English, German, or French, or wander through Berlin on their own. A detailed on-site map will prevent them from getting lost while they view the Berlin Wall, Brandenburg Gate, and other historic buildings and landmarks.

Bitburg American High School

http://www.brus-dso.odedodea.edu/schools/biths/bhshome.htm

These high school students of American armed services personnel want to take you on a tour of their school and of Bitburg, in western Germany, near the Luxembourg border. Before starting out, you may want to take their road sign test, to make sure you drive safely. Then let the students introduce you to the newspapers, history, and culture of Bitburg and the surrounding Eifel region. (Most of the information is found under *Our Community*.) Although the students don't furnish many graphics, they provide links to local Web sites that do.

Bus Stops of Hannover

http://www.uestra.de/busstops/default.html

When you're on a virtual field trip, even the bus stops become an event, especially when you're in Hannover, Germany. As part of Hannover's "Art in the Public Sphere" project, nine designers were commissioned to create nine bus and tram stops for the city, all of which are presented on this tour. The intent of the project was to change the passive, empty experience of waiting for a bus into a sensory experience. Our favorite stop along the tour was Wolfgang Lubersheimer's creation, which features parabolic reflectors that allow you to hear the conversations of people at the bus stop across the street.

GREECE

See also Chapter 1—Ancient Athens and Ancient Civilizations.

http://www.hri.org/nodes/grmus.htm

This extensive tour covers almost every aspect of Hellenic civilization by providing access to the museums of Greece and Cyprus, ancient Greek philosophers and writers, and arts and music. The tour is far too extensive to include a description of all available materials, but navigation is easy and self-explanatory through such categories as art, history, maritime, natural history, theatrical museums, music, literature, and arts. Other self-descriptive paths provide access to the various Greek cities, islands, mountains, rivers and lakes, and scenes of everyday life, flora, and fauna.

HAITI

http://pasture.ecn.purdue.edu/~agenhtml/agenmc/haiti/haiti.html

Students of Purdue University in Indiana invite you on a tour of Haiti. When we took the tour we discovered that Haiti was the first republic in the world to be led by a person of African descent. We owe Jean-Jacques Dessaline our thanks: His victory over Napoleon forced the emperor to abandon his plans for control of Louisiana. In addition to learning local history and culture, the tour includes views of various Haitian landscapes, cities, and beaches. You can also listen to Haitian music, learn about voodoo, and enjoy the local cuisine. Be warned—you need good strong teeth to be able to eat griots (boiled then fried goat).

INDIA

http://pages.cthome.net/india2

Calcutta has taken hold of Robert Menefee, and he wants to share his fascination of the city with your students. He'll teach them some basic Bengalese words, and then it's off into the city. Maybe you'll be lucky enough to arrive during the festival of Holi, when everyone runs joyously through the streets throwing colored water and powder on each other, and you'll end up green and magenta. The tour is as sprawling and diverse as the great city itself. You'll meet Nobel Prize-winning poet Rabindranath Tagore and filmmaker Satyajit Ray; learn about local festivals; hear music and meet the street musicians of Calcutta; see the botanical gardens, rice paddies, and memorials; and stop in at the Royal Calcutta Turf Club to watch racing and cricket.

IRAN

http://isfahan.anglia.ac.uk:8200/isfahan.html

Take your students to Isfahan, one of 10 cities designated by UNESCO as a universal heritage. We recommend that you first stop by the Tour Shop and pick up a free map of the city's mosques, shrines, minarets, palaces, and bridges. If your students aren't too impatient, stay a bit longer and obtain a copy of the *Fundamental Concepts*, a primer on Islamic architecture. Then it's off on your tour, hosted by a professor at Britain's Anglia Polytech University, who will explain the relationship between Islam, architecture, and history while showing stunning interiors and exteriors of buildings.

ISRAEL

http://www1.huji.ac.il/njeru/open_screen2.htm

Israeli government officials will take your students on a tour of Jerusalem through various time periods. The tour includes buildings, prominent historical people, and works of art. Wear comfortable shoes because you'll be doing a lot of walking and, if you get hungry along the way, taste local dishes from several periods. If you want to blend in with the locals, there are descriptions of costumes from several eras.

JAPAN

See also Chapter 1—A-Bomb Museum and Chapter 5—Aquariums—Enoshima Aquarium.

American School in Japan

http://www.asij.ac.jp

The students attending the nearly century-old pre-kindergarten through twelfth grade American School in Japan (ASIJ) are eager to share their projects with your class. Students will tell you about their local traditions and culture, including Koto music, tea ceremonies, fashions, shodo (calligraphy), and flower arranging. Preschoolers, who come from 14 different countries, are involved in cooking classes where they are learning how to measure, mix, and read directions. Join them on their sweet potato digs and omochi (rice pounding) activities. The K–5 students, originally from 43 different countries, will take you on a tour of urban and rural Japan. Be sure to read their multimedia cultural dictionary to prepare for the trip. Middle and high school students are also very busy and, in addition to their numerous Web projects, they've produced school newspapers and magazines that will be of interest to all students.

Japan—Nagatsuka Elementary School

http://www.vector.co.jp/authors/VA001962/nagatuka/indexe.html

A major focus of students attending Japan's Nagatsuka Elementary School is the study of peace. Your students are invited to participate in the school's *1,000 Cranes* project, in which peace messages are exchanged on a worldwide basis. Perhaps the nuclear attack on Hiroshima has such a large impact on the students because their "schoolmaster" lived through the experience. He'll share his experiences with visitors to his school.

Tokugawa Art Museum

http://www.cjn.or.jp/tokugawa/index.html

Take your students to the Tokugawa Art Museum in Nyoya, Japan. This institution, the third oldest privately endowed museum in the country, preserves the holdings of the Owari branch of the Tokugawa family, who maintained the closest family and political ties to the ruling shoguns throughout the Edo period (1603–1868). The collection, centered around objects inherited from the first shogun, Ieyasu, includes 8 designated national treasures, 50 registered important cultural properties, and 44 important art objects such as warrior saddles and armor from the sixteenth century, mirrors and chests from the private rooms of a shogun, a traditional noh theater stage and masks, and ceremonial tea objects. Narratives accompany each image. Be sure to take the time to view the grounds and garden tea houses.

JORDAN

http://www.kinghussein.gov.jo

Largely text-based, this tour of Jordan is devoted to the memory of King Hussein, who was the world's longest serving executive head of state. Either search for topics of interest or wander through the king's office, where you'll be directed to sections on history, geography, culture, government, tourist sites, and the economy. King Hussein's speeches, letters, interviews, and other documents may be found within the *Library*.

LAOS

See THAILAND

MYANMAR

See THAILAND

NICARAGUA
http://library.advanced.org/17749

English-, Spanish-, and Japanese-language tours of Nicaragua are available at this site. The tour is largely text-based, supplemented by audio interviews, music, photographs, and video clips. Teachers should be aware that, although portions of the tour are suitable for students of all ages, relatively controversial topics such as the Contra drug scandal are discussed. The tour begins with a detailed history of the country from the time of colonization and emphasizes eras of instability, oppression, and disaster such as the 1972 Managua earthquake and the Sandinista Revolution. You'll be introduced to people who played and continue to serve important roles in the country, such as activist Arnoldo Aleman and Violeta Chamorro, the woman who served as president from 1990 to 1996. Other portions of the tour include local culture (including sheet music for the national anthem) and economics.

NORTH POLE   PG
http://www.the-north-pole.com

Is there a better place than the North Pole for children to celebrate the holiday season? Santa will allow your students to peek into his mail bag and see what other kids from around the world have written. He'll even share some of his favorite crafts and recipes such as kissing boughs, origami ornaments, Mrs. Claus's favorite lime pie, and Rudolph's peanut butter oat treats. There are music and lyrics for carols and for games such as "Name That Tune" and the "Great North Pole Race." Feel free to hop in Santa's sleigh for a celebration of *Christmas Around the World.* He'll take you to over 30 countries, from Australia to Wales, to see how kids throughout the world celebrate Christmas. Be sure to send Rudolph and the elves some e-mail to let them know how you enjoyed your trip.

RUSSIA
See also Chapter 1—Soviet Union and Chapter 9—Photography and Photojournalism—Focal Point Photojournalist Group.

The Kremlin
http://www.moscowkremlin.ru/basic/english

English- or Russian-speaking guides will take you on a virtual tour of Moscow's Kremlin, with its dozens of towers, cathedrals, palaces, churches, monuments, and memorials. You can relax afterwards and venture outside the Kremlin for some shopping at the famous Moscow department store GUM.

Window to Russia

http://www.neuro.sfc.keio.ac.jp/~saito/sfc/meshi/stpeter.html

Window to Russia, a Moscow-based project by Relcom Corporation, provides access to a variety of resources from and about Russia. The hosts have provided an interactive Russian-English dictionary because some of the resources are available only in Russian. The tour includes information and images of Soviet documents, an introduction to Victor Bogorad (St. Petersburg's top cartoonist), and side trips to the Paleontology Institute of the Russian Academy of Science.

SINGAPORE

http://www.museum.org.sg/nhb/

The National Heritage Board of Singapore will take your students on a tour of the country's Asian Civilizations Museum, Singapore History Museum, and Singapore Art Museum and National Archives. By the time they're through, students will have seen textiles, garments, and art and artifacts from all of southeast Asia, China, India, and the Islamic world from ancient to contemporary times. The History Museum provides a context for the works, tracing historical trends and developments that have shaped the life of the country through demographics, social identification, festivals, trade, and commerce. The holdings of the National Archives include public records, building plans, oral history recordings, photographs, and movies. Of particular interest is the *Historic Sites Unit*, which takes students on a virtual tour of the country's national treasures, memorials and statues, and conservation areas.

SPAIN

http://www.docuweb.ca/SiSpain

The Spanish Embassy in Canada has provided this interactive service to "promote the free exchange of information on Spanish current affairs and arts, historical, linguistic, and cultural development." There is extensive information on virtually every topic, including geography, demographics, history, language, culture, politics, economics, infrastructure, and government. If you want to learn Spanish, they will direct you to appropriate sites. The entire tour is available in English, French, German, or Spanish.

THAILAND

http://www.asiatour.com/thailand/content1.htm

Take your students on a field trip to Thailand, where they will be able to attend various festivals, tour the county and its sites, and meet local people. The tour allows students to prepare for their trip by studying entry regulations, currency, health issues, transportation, and cuisine. You might want to check the *map room* for detailed maps of Thailand and nearby countries. Tours of Cambodia, Laos, Myanmar, Vietnam, and Yunnan are also available.

TURKEY

http://www.discoverturkey.com

Although this tour is conducted from a strongly partisan Turkish point of view, there is still much to see and do during your travels. Tour guides will cover Turkish history, carpets, culture, and government and even play the Turkish National Anthem and Mozart's *Turkish March* for you. You may wish to bypass information about Cyprus, as well as the first highlighted section of this tour, which proclaims how the Greek government sponsors international terrorism.

UNITED STATES

Post Office

http://www.usps.gov

Through rain, sleet, and snow, the United States Postal Service manages to deliver 107 billion pounds of first class mail per year. Every year, mail carriers drive 1.1 billion miles and process 38 billion changes of address. And they still have time to take your students on this interactive tour. Students will have the opportunity to use the official rate calculator to find out how much it costs to send that special birthday gift to a friend and follow their packages across the country with the express tracking system. Stamp lovers will have the chance to design their own stamp, learn about starting a collection, and find out why and how stamps are chosen—and why some will never be. There are also games, collections of letters to Santa, love letters, and even letters from presidents as far back as Washington. To find topics of interest, use the search engine function.

UNITED STATES—ALASKA

See also Chapter 4—Alaskan Wildflowers and Chapter 12—Sports—Dog Sledding.

Alaskan North Borough School District

http://www.nsbsd.k12.ak.us

Although students of the northernmost school district in the United States attend schools spread over 88,000 square miles, they are bound together by Inupiat cultural traditions. As a result of the geographic distances and weather conditions, students have developed a number of collaborative Internet projects, many of which involve local life-styles, flora, and fauna. Mabel Frankson will tell you, for example that it isn't really dark six months of the year: "It's more dark blue. We lose sun, not light." Others will show you what a year in the Arctic is like and how local people and plants depend on each other for survival.

UNITED STATES—CALIFORNIA

See also Chapter 6—California Living Museum and Chapter 7—Science—Museums and Laboratories—San Diego Natural History Museum.

Alcatraz Island

http://www.nps.gov/alcatraz

This tour of California's Alcatraz Island is conducted by the United States National Park Service. Alcatraz, originally known as La Isla de los Alcatracas (pelicans), has had many identities and functions through the centuries, most of which resulted from the island's isolation. The hosts will describe the military, penal, and Native American issues in historical contexts and answer such questions as why the penitentiary closed.

California Missions

http://www.escusd.k12.ca.us/EUSD.Home.html

Follow the kids of the Escondido, California, School District along the *Mission Internet Trail.* The elementary school students will take you through 21 historic missions from San Diego to San Francisco as part of a project they developed for an Internet cyberfair. Along the way, they'll share their knowledge of history and Native Californians. Students have thoughtfully provided narratives, photographs, audio materials, and even blueprints. Choose *Special Projects* to see what other things the students have been working on.

Los Angeles River

http://www.lalc.k12.ca.us/target/units/river/tour/index.html

The high school student who created this tour tells us that many people have never heard of the Los Angeles River. This trip allows digital navigation of the 50-mile river from its headwaters in the San Fernando Valley to its mouth in Long Beach. Along the way, the host shows you the local sights, plants, animals, and architecture, while sharing local information and history.

UNITED STATES—HAWAII

Kaumuali'i Elementary School

http://tqjunior.advanced.org/3502

The kids from Kaumuali'i Elementary School will teach you about Hawaiian legends, plants, wildlife, and history through this interactive game (the game will not work with the Internet Explorer browser). Those who would rather not walk the Kukui Trail can visit other parts of the site, where the students will show them how to make a surfboard; teach names, days, months, and numbers in Hawaiian; or introduce them to an Hawaiian ukulele master. If your class (or administration) is inspired to do a similar Internet project at your school, the kids have included lots of tips and tools they've used in constructing their own projects.

UNITED STATES—MISSOURI

St. Louis—Jefferson Expansion Memorial

See also Chapter 1—United States—Nineteenth Century.

http://www.nps.gov/jeff

Pay a visit to the Jefferson Expansion Memorial, courtesy of the United States National Park Service. Students will not only be able to see the St. Louis arch, courthouse, and the Museum of Westward Expansion, but they will also find equations used in calculating the curve of the arch and learn about the importance of the "keystone" in arch construction.

UNITED STATES—NEW ENGLAND

Covered Bridges

http://william-king.www.drexel.edu/top/bridge/cb1.html

Roger McCain, a professor of economics at Drexel University, wants to take your students on a tour of the covered bridges of southeastern Pennsylvania, New Jersey, Maryland, and Delaware. McCain sees the old "kissing bridges" as a reminder of a time "when life was simpler and closer to the land," and his love for the bridges is evident. Your students may wonder why bridges were covered, and McCain explains this and many other facts. Students can choose to tour by county or structural type. We recommend the *Photographic Essay* section, which combines historical data and local lore. There are images of covered bridges in every season, as well as links to other tours that delve deeper into engineering topics.

UNITED STATES—NEW JERSEY

New Jersey—Bergen Academies

http://www.bergen.org/AAST/projects/index.shtml

You wouldn't believe what the students of Bergen County, New Jersey's, magnet schools have been working on. This site highlights several of the schools' projects in humanities, sciences and math, and technology, some of the most innovative and intense uses of the Internet that we've seen. See the class of 2001's Rapid Prototype Project, in which they simulated the creation of a new corporation formed to produce, market, and sell paint to the public. Humanities projects include the "International Bazaar" (a virtual trip around the world), multimedia projects dealing with the Cold War, the Depression, explorers, American immigration, the Vietnam War, World War II, and even the Yiddish language. The sciences and math groups teamed with the Smithsonian Institution for a project on bio-visualization and also share their projects on the automobile's impact on the environment, three-dimensional math graphs, and their online physics textbooks. The technology group shares various technical tutorials, animations, and design projects, and all of the groups joined together to create the "Manhattan Project."

UNITED STATES—NEW YORK

Cayuga Heights Elementary School

http://www.icsd.k12.ny.us/cayugaheights

The students of Ithaca's Cayuga Heights Elementary School have been working hard on their energy project. Your students can participate in learning about the past and present uses of electricity and gas by reading a story from an 1852 utility booklet, finding 10 energy uses (if you can't find them, Cayuga students will give you the answers), and using math to try to calculate a gas bill in 1859. If you have time, stop by and meet the staff and students.

Central Park

http://www.centralpark.org/home.html

There are more than 50 places to explore on this self-guided tour of the United States' first landscaped park. Students are able to wander through Central Park's zoos and gardens and study its monuments at their leisure, while learning about the park's history. If you tire of wandering the park's 843 acres, sit back and watch the video.

Dr. Charles R. Drew Magnet School

http://drew.buffalo.k12.ny.us

Imagine the projects you could do if your school were located in a science museum or next door to a zoo! The Charles R. Drew Magnet School has three buildings, linked via a computer network. Pre-schoolers, kindergartners, and first grade students are housed in one of the buildings. They look forward to attending grades 2–6, which are held at the Buffalo Museum of Science. Seventh and eighth graders are in a building located on the grounds of the Buffalo Zoological Gardens and attend "zoo classes" every day. All of the students are proud of their school and anxious to share their projects and online lessons with your class. Be sure to read the inspirational story the students wrote about the school's namesake, recipient of several awards, including the NAACP's Spingarn Medal in 1944.

UNITED STATES—OHIO

Olmsted Middle School

http://www.ofcs.k12.oh.us/middle/hunt/hunt.html

Students and staff at the Olmsted Middle School are proud of their reputation for being at the forefront of technology, and invite classrooms throughout the world to participate in their *Internet Hunts*. Olmsted students spend five class periods working in teams that compete in the hunts, each of which has 10 questions that must be answered using resources available on the World Wide Web. Those less familiar with the Internet might want to read the school's *Surfing the Internet* manual. Your class is also invited to participate in developing future hunts. Click on "Technology Education" for details.

UNITED STATES—OREGON

Bridges

http://www.bizave.com/portland/bridges/Portland-Bridges.html

The first bridge across the Willamette River was constructed in 1887. Since that time, approximately two dozen other automobile and railroad bridges have been constructed across both the Willamette and Columbia Rivers. Students can tour these structures and learn how they were built, while absorbing some interesting Pacific Northwest history.

Buckman Elementary Magnet Arts School

http://buckman.pps.k12.or.us/buckman.html

Your students are welcome to enter each of the grades 1–5 classrooms at this Portland magnet school and see what the students have been learning. Buckman focuses on integrating the arts into all curricular areas.

Among their many other accomplishments, students have written a book that has been published by the city of Portland Water Bureau and have been interviewed by the Southprint Radio Series about their monarch butterfly project. Even with all of these activities, they still find the time to communicate with others over the Internet in real time using high-tech cameras. We recommend a visit to teacher Susan Verheyleweghen's class to see what kids with learning disabilities can do with the Internet.

Vose Elementary School

http://www.beavton.k12.or.us/vose/home.html

Beaverton, Oregon's, Vose Elementary School holds the distinction of being the first school in the Pacific Northwest built in a circular shape. Vose continues to find new ways to use the Internet. Among their other activities, the K–5 students have developed an online "kidopedia," an interactive encyclopedia with articles contributed by students throughout the world. The articles are browsable by topic or letter. See how you can contribute to the work, and be sure to visit the *Featured Vose Classroom*, featuring a variety of alternating student works. Not only do they post students' writings and artwork, but now you can actually hear students read their works and occasionally play an instrument.

UNITED STATES—WASHINGTON

Fairhaven Middle School

http://wwwfms.bham.wednet.edu

Explore this Bellingham, Washington, school's virtual museum and experience life in turn-of-the-century Fairhaven, at one time the salmon capital of the world. Visit various late-1800s buildings such as the purple castle. You're certain to run into people from all walks of life, from loggers to politicians, and the students offer instruction on how to create your own virtual museum.

Washington—Kulshan Middle School

http://wwwkms.bham.wednet.edu/lobby.htm

Pay a visit to the Pacific Rim Museum of Culture, established by the students of Bellingham, Washington's, Kulshan Middle School. A variety of documents and artifacts deal with the cultural diversity of the Pacific Rim, with a focus on the culture of middle schools and their students.

UNITED STATES—WASHINGTON, D.C.

Capital Tour

http://sc94.ameslab.gov/tour/tour.html

Take your students on a tour of our nation's capital. Detailed maps of the city and its subway system are provided, along with directions to each of the attractions. Included in the tour are such landmarks and cultural institutions as the Jefferson Memorial, the Ford Theater, the Federal Bureau of Investigation, and the Lincoln Memorial.

Congress and Senate

http://house.gov

Students can visit Congress and learn about the legislative process, who's who in the House of Representatives, and how to contact members by e-mail or "snail mail." Those interested in current events will be able to find the latest updates on pending bills and amendments. Your class can also pay a visit to the Senate at *http://www.senate.gov.*

White House

http://www.whitehouse.gov

Pay a visit to the president, his family, and the White House. Feel free to wander from room to room, learning about history, furnishings, and current events. The *Virtual Library* contains documents dating back to the start of the Clinton Administration, including transcripts of the president's radio addresses and executive orders. Be sure to stop by the *Briefing Room* for the day's press releases and the most up-to-date federal statistics. Younger students can take a special tour, where they'll meet pets and kids who have inhabited the famous structure. There is also a quarterly newsletter addressing such topics as crime, drugs, and poverty, in language geared toward grade school children.

VIETNAM

See also Thailand, Chapter 9—Photography and Photojournalism—Focal Point Photojournalist Group, and Chapter 10—Theater—Miss Saigon.

http://www.vietvet.org/visit.htm

Vietnam War veterans will take your students on a tour of Vietnam and share their views of the changes that have transpired in the country since the war. The vets' observations about Vietnam range from reminiscences to tips for travelers. A language primer is also provided.

WALES
http://www.castlewales.com/home.html

Jeff Thomas, a castle enthusiast, will escort your class through over 100 castles and abbeys, while providing knowledge that imparts a genuine feeling for what life inside a castle was really like. For example, Thomas explains such things as the ingenious construction of fireplaces and how they were designed to spread heat the maximum distance. He also covers pre-castle Welsh history and provides an historical timeline, as well as a glossary and bibliography.

WORLD-WIDE TOUR
http://www.castlesontheweb.com

Ted Monk, a castle enthusiast, will take your students on guided tours of dozens of castles, palaces, homes, abbeys, and churches throughout the world. From Austria to Yugoslavia, students will be able to walk through each of the structures, learning history and other subjects along the way. We suggest that you supervise this tour, as it is largely composed of links to other sites on the Internet.

YUNNAN
See THAILAND

CHAPTER 3

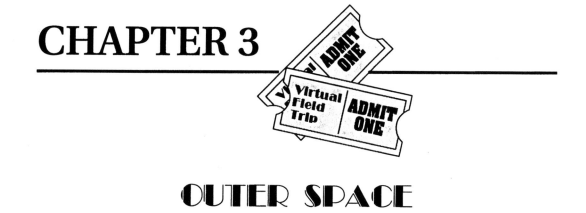

OUTER SPACE

See also Chapter 7—Science—Aviation and Aerospace and Science—Museums and Laboratories—Children's Museum of Indianapolis.

Why not pay a visit to the final frontier? Institutions such as NASA and the Los Alamos National Laboratory will be more than happy to accompany your class to the sun, Jupiter, Mars, outer galaxies, and black holes. The less adventuresome may want to stay behind and visit some virtual laboratories or view outer space through robotic telescopes.

ARTY THE ASTRONAUT   PG
http://www.artyastro.com

Arty and his friend Gregor, boys by day and astronauts by night, are eager to take your students on a tour of the solar system. Not only do they need someone to act as captains, but they love to share their extensive knowledge of the solar system through interactive multimedia games and quizzes, as well as brief narrative information. Students can see how much they weigh and how fast they age on each planet and play games that develop hand-eye coordination and keyboard skills. Good sound effects and animation, plus a log-on system that personalizes each student's trip, make this a fun educational field trip.

ASTRONOMY FOR KIDS
http://tqjunior.advanced.org/3645

Twelve-year-old New Hampshire students Stephen, Ben, and Jeff have developed this tour under the supervision of their sixth-grade teacher. Your students can peer through their virtual telescope and visit black holes, constellations, the planets, and the stars and share their thoughts and questions with students throughout the world. Find out why stars twinkle and whether the universe will ever end. This is an excellent example of how teachers can help students combine the Internet with research.

BRADFORD ROBOTIC TELESCOPE
http://www.telescope.org/rti/index.html

The University of Bradford's Department of Industrial Technology has a robotic telescope mounted high on the moors in West Yorkshire. Anyone with Internet access is able to use the telescope to look at anything in the northern night sky. The university simply requires registration (free of charge), at which time you will be issued a user name and password. Requests are automatically prioritized and scheduled as time allows. In the meantime, you can look at pictures previously taken by the telescope, such as those of Comet Hyakutake and lunar eclipses.

CELESTIAL CARTOGRAPHY
http://www.lhl.lib.mo.us/pubserv/hos/stars/toc.htm

This tour explores the history of celestial cartography through star atlases and maps covering the period from 1482 to 1851. Although all five of the "Grand" celestial atlases are included, the focal point of the tour is Bayer's *Uranometria*, the first to allow star positions to be read to a fraction of a degree.

COSMO NET
http://library.advanced.org/27930/

Upper-level students will gain the most from this tour, although younger students will enjoy some of the views. All aspects of theoretical and observational cosmology are covered, including quantum mechanics, string theory, the Big Bang theory, and much more. The tour is text-based, with supplemental interactive games and quizzes.

CURIOSITY CLUB
http://www.sfusd.edu/curiosity_club/bridge1.html

The Curiosity Club at Sunnyside School in San Francisco collaborated with the Center for Extreme Ultraviolet Astrophysics in Berkeley, California, and the San Francisco Unified School District to study the collision of Comet Shoemaker-Levy 9 with Jupiter. Watch a movie of Sunnyside students "traveling" with NASA's EUV *Explorer* satellite and find out the answers to questions students are asking. Or, feel free to take your own tour of the *Explorer* while learning about the technology connected with Jupiter and comets. There is a link to an observatory with spectacular pictures of Jupiter and collisions, as well as glossaries and an astral gallery that has collision-inspired artwork created by students.

HANDS-ON UNIVERSE
http://hou.lbl.gov/

How many of your students question the practicality of algebra, geometry, and physics? This K–12 curriculum project, developed by the University of California at Berkeley's Lawrence Hall of Science (with support from the National Science Foundation and the United States Departments of Defense and Energy), answers these questions by taking your students on a tour of the galaxies. Students from around the world can request and download observations from telescopes and analyze images using various concepts of math, science, and technology. Teenagers at Northfield Mount Hermon and Oil City High Schools actually discovered a new planet! Teachers will want to take a pre-tour of the project overview and meet the staff, teacher resource agents, and project collaborators.

NATIONAL AERONAUTICS AND SPACE ADMINISTRATION (NASA)

NASA has such an extensive Web site that we have chosen to break it down into various sections to make your tour more efficient. Out of all the U.S. government agencies, NASA is perhaps the one to make the most use of the Internet, with tours for every age and level of expertise. There is a heavy focus on K–12 education, as well as the development of teacher knowledge and expertise. The tours listed below are some of our favorites. Feel free to explore NASA on your own, as there are many areas with lesson plans, teaching resources, grants, scholarships, workshops, and conferences.

Compton Gamma Ray Observatory
http://antwrp.gsfc.nasa.gov

Upper-grade students can tour the Compton Observatory Science Support Center, where they'll learn all about gamma ray astrology. Scientists will show them images of the universe from collapsed stars to the cores of black holes and share some of the latest discoveries resulting from this technology, such as bursting pulsars.

Jet Propulsion Observatory
http://galileo.jpl.nasa.gov

NASA's Jet Propulsion Laboratory has assembled a collection of the best images from the agency's planetary exploration program. There is precise, comprehensive information about the planets and moons in our solar system, as well as photographs of and information about the satellites that took and transmitted the images.

Lunar Prospector

http://lunar.arc.nasa.gov

Welcome to the moon! Students can not only tour the moon through this multimedia presentation but also virtually operate the *Lunar Prospector,* launched to the moon in 1998. It's a lot of responsibility. After a course on the *Prospector's* instrumentation, students will have to monitor its "health log," keeping track of the state of the antenna, battery, solar panels, fuel tank, and thrusters. Others may prefer to take in the interactive views of the moon or interpret data on three-dimensional maps. Teachers will want to view the Tools section before starting the tour—it provides the plug-ins needed for your computers.

NASA Kids

http://kids.msfc.nasa.gov

Kindergarten through eighth grade students are invited to join NASA's *Kid's Club* and visit this site as often as they wish. Tours of rockets, airplanes, and outer space are available just about any time you wish to go. For those who suffer from motion sickness, NASA has designed educational projects and games you can do from the comfort and safety of the classroom. There is a special *Teacher's Corner,* where students can design word searches; learn how to submit their stories and artwork to the site; and be informed of when they will be able to see shuttles, space stations, and other events. There is always a special kid's feature story involving new developments in science. Unfamiliar words are highlighted and linked to a glossary. A similar site, designed for high school students, may be found at *http://liftoff.msfc.nasa.gov.*

Observatorium

http://observe.ivv.nasa.gov/nasa/core.shtml.html

Stop by NASA's *Observatorium* for tours of the planets and stars of our solar system. Scientists will tell your students all about aeronautics, earth science, and space science through multimedia images and online activities. They have provided teacher's guides for each of the articles appearing on site.

Shuttle Countdown

http://www.ksc.nasa.gov/shuttle/countdown

Don't miss NASA's latest shuttle mission. *Shuttle Countdown* will keep you informed about upcoming space shuttle launches, processing, countdowns, and status. There are descriptions of various shuttles, as well as multimedia presentations of the history of the shuttle program, crews, and milestones. Tours of past missions are also available.

NINE PLANETS

http://www.seds.org/nineplanets/nineplanets/nineplanets.html

Bill Arnett, an astronomy buff, has compiled this comprehensive site on the planets and major moons of our solar system. The photographs alone are worth the trip, but the amount of information on each celestial body, ranging from technical data to cultural allusions, is equally impressive. The tour includes animation of such events as orbital paths and space probes, sound excerpts from such sources as Holst's *The Planets*, and links to related information.

NORTHERN LIGHTS PLANETARIUM

http://www.uit.no/npt/nordlyset/nordlyset.en.html

Travel to Norway for a stunning view of the Aurora Borealis. The tour is sponsored by Norway's first public and virtual planetarium. Some of the more technical information, such as Northern Lights physics, is presented only in Norwegian, but the pictures and movies are beyond language.

SOLAR SYSTEM LIVE

http://www.fourmilab.ch/solar/solar.html

Take a tour of the inner planets or the entire solar system, courtesy of Switzerland's John Walker. Students will have to do some work on this trip as they manipulate controls to set time, dates, points of observation, orbital elements, etc. Those whose computers are equipped with Windows are able to create displays in real time as they view the Earth, sky, and stars and track satellites. We even learned about the word "orrery."

SPACE TELESCOPE SCIENCE INSTITUTE

http://hubble.stsci.edu

View images from the Hubble telescope, courtesy of the Space Telescope Science Institute at Johns Hopkins. This multimedia presentation includes astronomical events such as galaxy formations, Neptune's rotation, and a dramatic example of the transformation of a star into a planetary nebula. There are numerous interactive K–12 classroom activities where students are able to construct the Milky Way, travel through black holes, and obtain solar system trading cards. Students may also enroll in *Deep Field Academy* as cadets. After completing coursework on careers as Stellar Statisticians, Cosmic Classifiers, and Galactic Guides, they'll take the final exam to become Universal Graduates.

THE SUN

Tour 1

http://sirius.astro.uva.nl/~michielb/sun/kaft.htm

Hop over to the University of Amsterdam for a 20-minute trip to the sun. Students will experience flames larger than 10 Earths and solar winds so powerful that they reach beyond Pluto. The end of the tour is somewhat disconcerting because it describes the sun's dying process and the eventual destruction of the Earth and the rest of the solar system. This award-winning tour is available in both English and Dutch.

Tour 2

http://library.thinkquest.org/15215

Your students will love this tour of the sun, accompanied by the sounds of the Beatle's "Here Comes the Sun." Designed by three teenagers, who collaborated from their homes in Alaska, New York, and India, there are special tours for grades 4–6 and 7–12, with hundreds of pages of information, graphics, and activities. Be sure to watch the movie and check out the *Sun Web Cam,* thoughtfully provided by the Solar and Heliospheric Observatory and the Mauna Loa Solar Observatory.

CHAPTER 4

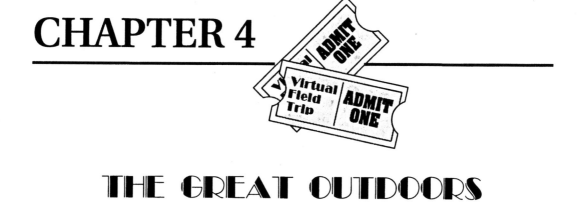

THE GREAT OUTDOORS

From the barren Death Valley to lush botanical gardens, your students can spend the day marveling at nature's wonders. Take a look at the world through the eyes of a bee, fly through the eye of a hurricane, or perform a virtual frog dissection. Be sure to check Mother Nature's handiwork in Chapter 6—Animal Kingdom and Chapter 5—Aquatic and Marine Life also.

ALASKAN WILDFLOWERS   PG
http://tqjunior.advanced.org/6274

A group of home-schooled students from the state of Alaska want to show you their favorite state wildflowers. They simply ask that you do not pick any of them, so that they will be available for others to see. In return, they'll take you through the alpine, lowland, and forest areas of Alaska on a tour that includes photographs, information, recipes using flowers, explanations of the life cycle of the flowers, and activities and quizzes geared toward primary grades.

BIRD WATCHING

Audubon's Birds of America
http://employeeweb.myxa.com/rrb/Audubon/index.html

If you want information about any bird residing in the Americas, here's the place to start. All seven volumes of John James Audubon's original *Birds of America* (1840–1844), including sections on state and extinct birds, are here. And, unlike reading the original book, your students can actually hear many of the birdcalls.

Backyard Birding

http://www.slivoski.com/birding

Bird lovers Janet and John Slivoski invite your students to their Indiana home to take a look at the dozens of feathered visitors that frequent their back yard. Simply click on the name of the bird for a brief description. Photographs, videos, and sound clips are available for several of the birds, and more are constantly being added. If you have time, you're welcome to take a look at some of the butterflies that also hang out in the Slivoskis' back yard.

Birding Southern Queensland

http://server.ats.com.au/~aviceda

There's a lot of territory to cover in Queensland, Australia, and a lot of birds. There are 16 photos of cuckoos alone, and even some shots of the rare pellagra. The many tours are uneven—some are heavily visual, some mostly textual—so you may have to go on a few trips to both see and learn about Queensland's birds. After taking Tom and Marie's many bird watching trips, you're welcome to try their bird identification quiz and e-mail your answers. Part of the Australia Birding Web Ring, a consortium of birders linked on the Internet, Tom and Marie will direct you to birding links throughout Australia and the world. There are even birding tours of Saudi Arabia.

Birds of Arizona

http://www.mirror-pole.com

This extensive collection of images, texts, and sound recordings is the result of work conducted on the state government's *Arizona Breeding Bird Atlas*. The diversity of Arizona's climate and topography results in a stunning variety of birds, from the desert roadrunner to the mountain blue bird. Primary grade students will love the comparison photos of baby, juvenile, and adult chipping sparrows, each perched on someone's hand. Local students can help track the paths and numbers of the Peach Faced Lovebird, a native of West Africa that poses a danger of taking over nesting places used by native birds.

Eagles

http://www.eagles.org

The National Foundation to Protect America's Eagle (NFPAE) presents an overview of the 59 species of eagles found throughout the world, with an emphasis on those found within the United States. There are fact sheets, photographs, and audio clips of eagle sounds, and even the lyrics to the "Save the Eagle Song" recorded by some of country and western music's greats. Information on how your school can adopt an eagle is also included.

Feral Monk Parakeets in Chicago

http://home.uchicago.edu/~jmsouth

Chicago's Hyde Park neighborhood is best known as home to the University of Chicago, but Jason South has designed this tour to introduce you to a resident hardier and more adaptable than even U of C students: the monk parakeet. Monk parakeets successfully nest and breed in an intemperate urban environment, building nests under utility wires (possibly for warmth) and often sharing space with squirrels. They were first spotted in Hyde Park in 1973, and by 1979 they were successfully nesting and breeding. It is interesting to note that these birds, native to Argentina and Brazil, have learned to adapt to inclement Chicago winters. Mr. South has mapped and photographed the birds and their nesting sites and provides information on their diets, foraging habits, and the political controversy they have created.

Owls

http://www.owlpages.com

Because of their excellent sight and hearing and their ability to fly silently, owls are the lords of twilight and night. This tour, conducted by a group of international owl enthusiasts, sheds light on every conceivable facet of these fascinating birds. Whether you're interested in physiological facts, rehabilitation efforts, habits, or mythology, you'll find photos, diagrams, and information on this tour, including recordings of bird calls.

Penguins

http://home.capu.net/~kwelch/penguins

This primarily text-based tour is geared toward upper-level students. Younger students should stick to the *Penguin Species* portion of the tour, where there are photographs, movies, and audio recordings of the world's 16 penguin species. Other, more technical areas cover such topics as evolution, ethology, and biology correlates. Each section begins with a basic primer and then becomes progressively more technical. This is an excellent tour for upper-level biology classes.

Peterson's Online Birds

http://www.petersononline.com

Who better to learn the art of bird watching from than Roger Tory Peterson, author of the noted *Peterson's Guide to North American Birds*? In addition to Peterson's tips, there are approximately two dozen birds covered in this tour, with text and photographs from the *Peterson CD ROM* published by Houghton-Mifflin. For each of the North American birds listed Peterson's artwork; a life history of the bird; a seasonal range map; and information about similar species, physical characteristics, habitat, nests, and conservation are included. The tour also includes selected material from the *Bird Watchers Digest*.

FALL FOLIAGE
http://www.fallinpa.com

If you can't find the time for a leisurely drive up the eastern seaboard, this virtual tour of Pennsylvania's foliage is ideal. The colors are so vibrant that locals call the drive "the big Pennsylvania fireworks show." While you're watching the leaves change, you'll learn how to identify various trees by their leaves, twigs, fruit, and bark. A quicktime movie shows the trees rapidly changing from summer to fall. Primary grade students will want to pay a visit to the playground, where they can color in the foliage on-screen.

INSECTS

See also Chapter 7—Science—Microscopy, Science—Museums and Laboratories—Field Museum of Natural History, and Science—Museums and Laboratories—Yuckiest Site on the Internet.

Bee Eye
http://cvs.anu.edu.au/andy/beye/beyehome.html

Australian neuroscientist Andrew Giger's *Bee Eye* allows your students to see the world through the eyes of a honeybee. Students can hover at close range, get a "full-scope" view, or work the on-site software for various magnifications and other parameters.

The Bug Club   `PG`
http://www.ex.ac.uk/bugclub

Students in the biology department at the University of Exeter in the United Kingdom are looking for kids who "want to cuddle a cockroach, stroke a stick insect, or hug a harvestman." Exeter's biology students will share articles, photographs, games, and puzzles. Students can also find pen pals who are interested in bugs and learn how to keep various insects as pets. Being Green, they remind kids, isn't just about recycling; it's about caring for insects as well.

Butterflies
http://library.thinkquest.org/C002251/index2.shtml

Fourteen- to seventeen-year-old students from Germany, Singapore, and the United States will transport your students into the world of butterflies. We're told that the life of a butterfly is all about changes, and this multimedia presentation takes us through the butterfly life cycle as it is nourished, escapes from predators, and changes form. Along the way, find out where silk comes from, watch butterfly migration (some can fly as fast as 37 miles per hour), and learn how to develop your own butterfly garden. There are interactive activities, quizzes, and instructions for creating your own paper butterfly (with or without scales). Tours are available in English, German, and Chinese.

Entomology Image Gallery

http://www.ent.iastate.edu/imagegallery

The Department of Entomology at Iowa State University has dozens of pictures and movies about ticks, beetles, mosquitoes, lice, and other insects common to the Midwest. We're certain your class will enjoy the sequence of pictures that show "the dissecting of the midgut from a partially engorged adult female deer tick." For anyone who's ever been tormented by mosquitoes, here's a chance to watch scientists return the favor.

Insecta Inspecta World

http://www.insecta-inspecta.com

Students of Fremont, California's, Thornton Jr. High School Honors Academy spent a year delving into the world of insects and are eager to take your class to *Insecta Inspecta World.* The students believe that since the world is covered with bugs, it is beneficial to get to know about them, and they will tell you about the world of insects, from ants to termites. In addition to photographs and narratives, students, under the review of the Smithsonian's National Museum of Natural History, investigate the benefits and drawbacks of each insect. For example, although the African termite is an important food source, it is also responsible for one-fifth of the world's methane gas. The site is heavily textual, but because it's written by students, the language is friendly and lively. Students tired of all the information—and there's a lot of it—can check out the winners of Bugfest 2000 in the art gallery, to which students across the country submitted drawings of insects.

Worms   PG

http://www.urbanext.uiuc.edu/worms/

Squirmin' Herman the worm has written a multimedia autobiography that he'd like to share with your students. Beginning with his ancestral migration on a seventeenth-century wooden ship, Herman's story includes a climb up his family tree; a study of his body; and a tour of his neighborhood haunts, such as *Whole Worm Foods* and the *Book Worm Library.* There are activities for students and a special teacher's bin with lesson plans and suggested resources.

LAKE BIG FISH—A BACKYARD HABITAT

http://www.cirr.com/~gensie

Lake Big Fish in Plano, Texas, which is more of a suburban pond than an actual lake, has been certified as a "backyard habitat" by the National Wildlife Federation. In addition to your students seeing the "lake" in summer, fall, winter, and spring and learning about the birds, honeysuckle, and other animal and plant life, this is a lesson in urban ecology, alerting students that nature exists and can be appreciated, nurtured, and protected, even in unlikely places. Liz Gensheimer, your host, will tell you how to find your own backyard habitat and get it certified.

PARKS AND SANCTUARIES
See also Chapter 2—Australia.

Australian Botanic Gardens

http://155.187.10.12/anbg/index.html

Canberra's Australian Botanic Gardens displays a wide diversity of plants native to the continent, from the rainforests of eastern Australia to the alpine and desert regions. Tour guides will accompany your students, explaining each of the plants, how to grow them, and how they are used by native aboriginals. If you're quiet, you may be lucky enough to get a close look at Australian birds and frogs. Keep an eye out for the Gripps-land Water Dragon, who looks fierce but is really shy.

Death Valley

http://www.nps.gov/deva

Make sure you have plenty of water for this trip to Death Valley—it has the hottest climate in North America. The United States National Park Service (NPS) takes you along the hiking trails and back roads of this 3.3-million-acre national monument, teaching about desert safety, biology, and geology. Be sure to visit some of the ghost towns such as Panamint City ("the toughest, rawest, most hard-boiled little hellhole that ever passed for a civilized town"). In return for telling you how to get there, the NPS asks that your students respect "every piece of rusting machinery and bit of wood—they represent a part of our past."

Grand Canyon National Park

http://www.kaibab.org

Referring to the Grand Canyon, President Theodore Roosevelt once said, "Do nothing to mar its grandeur for the ages have been at work upon it and man cannot improve it. Keep it for your children, your children's children, and all who come after you." But he never imagined that it could be preserved and presented over the Internet, so that millions of people could view it from their homes and schools. Your guided tour is complete with maps, history, scenic photographs, and articles. Students can also learn how to become junior rangers and how to make split twig figurines, works of art dating back 4,000 years to the forebears of the Anasazi culture.

John Muir Trail

http://www.reiseagentur.de/JMT/JMTTitel.html

Dr. Stefan Krempl, an international chemist and avid outdoorsman, will take your class on a walk along the John Muir Trail from Tuolowme Meadows in Yosemite to Mt. Whitney. The site is short on text but has stunning photographs.

Sequoia and Kings Canyon National Park

http://www.nps.gov/seki/index.htm

The second oldest national park in the United States was established in 1890 to protect trees in the Great Forest. The National Park Service will share such natural wonders as the General Sherman Tree (the world's largest living thing) and Mt. Whitney, the highest mountain in the United States outside of Alaska.

Yellowstone National Park

http://www.nps.gov/yell/index.htm

The National Park Service will take you through the United States' first and oldest national park, showing such natural wonders as geysers and Yellowstone Falls, while explaining how these geographic features originally occurred. They've provided coloring books and activities for younger students, a scavenger hunt for older students, and technical information for more advanced students.

RAINFOREST

http://www.euronet.nl/users/mbleeker/suriname/suri-eng.html

Jan Hein Ribot of the Netherlands will take your students on a tour of the tropical rainforest in Suriname, an island near Venezuela. Through text (available in 10 languages), photographs, and sounds, students will experience plant, animal, and tribal life in the forest. They'll even be able to attend a marriage ceremony and gain an understanding of local culture. The Caribs, for example, were responsible for the invention of sailing ships, yet, to this day, they do not make use of the wheel.

VOLCANOES

Michigan Tech University

http://www.geo.mtu.edu/volcanoes

Michigan Tech University, in cooperation with the Keweenaw Volcano Observatory, has compiled an ongoing database of current and historical volcanic activity for every volcanic range on Earth, including satellite and ground photographs. Tours include articles on volcanic research, remote sensing, safety tips, and eruptive products. There is even a section on volcano humor which, as you might expect, is quite short.

Volcano World

http://volcano.und.nodak.edu

Travel to the world's volcanoes, including those on the moon and Mars. Through high-quality remote sensing images, interactive experiments, and other materials, students can see what's currently erupting, learn how to build models and become volcanologists, and visit parks and monuments.

 WEATHER

Cloud Boutique

http://vortex.plymouth.edu/clouds.html

Pay a visit to The Weather Center at New Hampshire's Plymouth College, lie back, and watch cloud formations roll across the sky. Researchers will explain the various clouds and show your students a 30-minute time-lapse video loop showing how clouds move and change shape.

Hurricane Hunters

http://www.hurricanehunters.com

"Teal Four One, Keesler Tower. Cleared for takeoff, runway two one." You are about to take one of the most frightening and educational airplane rides of your life as you fly through the eye of a hurricane with the Air Force Reserve's 53rd Weather Reconnaissance Squadron (aka The Hurricane Hunters). Captain Lance Oakland will provide your pre-flight briefing and issue equipment (ear plugs are essential), and then it's off into Hurricane Opal. During the flight you'll learn about this meteorological phenomenon and learn how to interpret reconnaissance reports. Have a safe flight!

Hurricane Storm Science Center

http://www.miamisci.org/hurricane

Personnel of the Miami Science Center will take your students inside a hurricane and explain the science behind these powerful storms. Students will learn how to make a hurricane spiral and use tools to measure air pressure, weather conditions, and moisture. *Killer Storms* will teach students about hurricane tracking, storm warnings, safety rules, and how to make a hurricane shopping list, while the *Healing Quilt* allows people to share stories of weather disasters.

CHAPTER 5

AQUATIC AND MARINE LIFE

See also Chapter 7—Museums and Laboratories—San Diego Natural History Museum.

Boot up, sit back, and let us take you from a Massachusetts tide pool to the deep ocean. Along the way, you'll see the fresh water dolphins of the Amazon, swim with sharks, and hear the songs of whales and dolphins. Walk around aquariums from the United States and Japan or dive to the bottom of the sea in submarines. If you still have time, relax by scuba diving in Maui, where you'll also learn about underwater photography. After all, without photos, who's going to believe the amazing places you've been?

 AQUARIUMS

Enoshima Aquarium

http://www.imasy.org/~mtoyokaw/enoshima

Japan's Enoshima Aquarium invites you to see the sea otters, dolphins, jellyfish, and other sea creatures that reside in the aquarium and the surrounding waters. Viewing a foreign aquarium affords a unique perspective. For example, a collection of photographs of people touching some of the fish and dolphins carries this caption: "To become familiar with animals promotes the nurturing of the emotions and it provides a very good influence in character building, especially for children. Many kinds of efforts are being made so that visitors . . . feel a kind of skin contact."

Florida Aquarium

http://www.flaquarium.net

Folks from the Florida Aquarium will take your students on a tour of the state's natural habitats, following the life cycle of a drop of water through a local mangrove forest, out to the bays and beaches, to the coral reef, and offshore—all while viewing and learning about local wildlife. There are experiments for "wannabe marine biologists of all ages," a *Play*

Pond where knowledge of natural Florida can be tested, and games such as *Critter Match*. Be sure to check out the 360-degree panoramic view of the coral reef.

Gulf of Maine Aquarium

http://octopus.gma.org

This Gulf of Maine Aquarium tour focuses on the state's unique range of aquatic environments, which include fresh and saltwater habitats streams, ponds, bogs, tidepools, beaches, and aquifers. But it also links to real-time world-wide adventures. Your class can, for example, ride along with the deep-sea diving *Alvin* as it researches thermal vents and volcanoes, or participate in a whale search. Each trip—local or abroad—includes suggestions for classroom activities. Students can learn to read a watershed map or research the myths behind the names of modern research vessels like the *Argos*. For another field trip aboard *Alvin,* see *Ocean Adventures.*

 # DOLPHINS

Amazon River Dolphins

http://www.virtualexplorers.org

Research biologist Tamara McGuinn invites your class to board her 76-foot wooden boat for a trip through Peru's Pacaya-Samiria Reserve to study fresh water river dolphins. Along the way, you'll learn how to determine what scientific data are needed and how to collect and interpret scientific findings. Although you'll be busy, there will still be time for trips to various villages along the river and in the Andes. Lesson plans and activities are also offered on site.

The Dolphin Institute

http://www.dolphin-institute.org

Hop on over to the islands and pay a visit to the denizens of Honolulu's Dolphin Institute. Students can listen to the residents "talk" to each other and learn about their cognitive and sensory systems, anatomy, and behavior. Each dolphin has its own vocal signature, and your class can listen to each and try to tell the difference. Be sure to visit the humpback whales while you're there. The Institute's tours are suitable for all ages.

MASSACHUSETTS TIDE POOL
http://www.umassd.edu/Public/People/Kamaral/thesis/tidepools.html

Kimberly Amaral shares her Dartmouth thesis, allowing students to learn all about plants and creatures residing in a typical Massachusetts tide pool. Using the on-site tide pool map, students click on any organism of interest, from arthropods to sea urchins. There are also projects for working with tide pool flora such as making seaweed prints. Surely, home economics teachers will appreciate the recipe for seaweed pudding.

OCEAN ADVENTURE
http://library.advanced.org/18828

Many refer to the ocean's depths as Earth's last frontier. There's a lot to think about before your students volunteer for this virtual tour on board the DSV *Alvin,* a submersible maintained and operated by the Woods Hole Oceanographic Institute in Massachusetts. Those with claustrophobia might want to skip the trip—three people will submerge 7,290 feet for eight hours in a vessel equivalent in size to a bathtub. There are also ethical considerations—administrators will present the pros and cons of ocean research and mining, but students will have to make the final decision themselves. There's an online forum where they are able to post their views and/or read the conclusions of others. Even if you choose not to board the ship, there are many things to keep you busy. Feel free to attend the multimedia dive briefing, where you can learn all about hydrothermal vents, or sit back and watch some of the most unusual and ancient forms of life on Earth, such as the giant tube worm and the eyeless shrimp. You may even find clues about the origins of life in our solar system. This is an unparalleled opportunity to learn from research assistants, marine geophysicists, microbiologists, geochemists, Benthic ecologists, and geologists. Be sure not to miss the interactive activities, including quizzes, mapping, and temperature conversion. And don't forget to print the certificate of completion of your virtual journey.

SCUBA DIVING IN MAUI
http://www.maui.net/~scuba/index.html

What better way to learn about underwater life than through scuba diving? Check out the current weather and sea conditions, choose your diving spot on the interactive map, and drop over the side. You'll swim with sharks, dolphins, and the smaller fellows such as Moorish idols and thread fin butterfly fish. Your hosts will also be happy to teach you how to take underwater photographs.

SEA TURTLE MIGRATION
http://www.cccturtle.org/sat1.htm

The "tears" shed by sea turtles are not a result of leaving their 80 to 120 young to hatch all by themselves. They are really secretions of excess salt accumulated from the hundreds of miles of migration through the sea. The Sea Turtle Survival League shares their extensive knowledge of these fascinating creatures and the efforts to protect them from extinction. Students can watch video clips and learn about the different species and their feeding, nesting, and mating behavior. Follow their movements via a regularly updated map with data from satellite tracking and pay a visit to the Archie Carr National Wildlife Refuge, where you can learn about the role of Florida's coastal habitats. A free teacher's guide incorporates math, biology, and art with resources on site.

SEA WORLD
http://www.seaworld.org

Pay a visit to Sea World and browse through their *Animal Information Database,* with photographs of and facts about almost all forms of aquatic life. While you're there, feel free to join the teams of research biologists as they travel throughout the world. They'll be happy to take you to Marion Island in South Africa to study and identify the migration patterns of elephant seals, or to Antarctica to study the Weddell seals. Others may prefer to follow the journeys of loggerhead turtles, observe African gorillas and elephants, take an *Aquatic Safari,* or just sit back and watch the *Penguin Cam* or browse the *Animal Sounds Library.* Teachers will want to check the many educational resources with lesson plans and other materials for grades K–12.

UNITED STATES COAST GUARD
http://www.uscg.mil

This award-winning official U.S. Coast Guard site has biographies, speeches, and information about the Coast Guard commandant, photographs, drawings, maps, and vessel and aircraft data sheets. The site is updated frequently with information about and pictures of the latest Coast Guard operations. Younger students will want to visit the *Kid's Corner,* which has an online coloring book with water safety tips and an audio recording of the Coast Guard anthem.

WHALES
See also Aquariums—Gulf of Maine Aquarium and Dolphins—The Dolphin Institute.

Charlotte the Vermont Whale

http://www.uvm.edu/whale/whalehome.html

In 1849 the fossil of a Beluga whale was found buried 10 feet below ground in the state of Vermont. Amazingly, Charlotte's resting spot was over 150 miles from the nearest ocean. Pay a visit to this exhibit to learn all about Beluga whales, fossil preservation, and glaciers.

WhaleNet

http://whale.wheelock.edu

WhaleNet, developed jointly by the biology departments of Wheelock and Simmons Colleges and the National Science Foundation, is one of the most complete Internet information sources on whales. Students can learn about whale tagging and satellite tracking, study maps showing migratory patterns, or download blank maps and recorded sightings and create their own maps. This tour also offers information and bibliographies on every species of whale and, if you don't find the information you need, scientists will answer your questions via e-mail. Tours are available in English, Spanish, Portuguese, German, and French. Teachers may want to visit this site ahead of time for lesson plans, activities, and links to online interactive books.

Whale's World

http://www.cs.sfu.ca/research/projects/Whales/

The *Virtual Whale's World Project* from Simon Fraser University in Canada is intended to be "an education and conservation tool to celebrate the lives of humpback whales." Sounds, movies, and three-dimensional animations enable visitors to experience the feeding behaviors of Pacific humpback whales. There is also dramatic underwater footage. The text on how pods of humpbacks trap and feed on schools of herrings should leave no doubt in anyone's mind about the intelligence of whales.

CHAPTER 6

ANIMAL KINGDOM

See also Chapter 1—International Horse Museum, Chapter 4—Bird Watching and Insects, Chapter 5—Sea World, and Chapter 11—Circus.

About the only thing your students can't do on our virtual visits to animals around the world is smell them. But they *will* be able to hear them growl and howl, and they can watch them hop, run, leap, and eat. Whether it's a virtual field trip to zoos, wildlife preserves, froggy swamps, savannas, or jungles, in Antarctica, Africa, Australia, or the United States, you're sure to meet and learn about whichever animal you're looking for.

 ## ANIMAL SOUNDS `PG`

http://www.georgetown.edu/cball/animals/animals.html

Cathy Ball of Georgetown University's Department of Linguistics wants to show your students how different languages can turn a simple cow's moo into the Tower of Babel. For example, although a bee may sound the same in Spain and Japan, the Spanish sound is translated as *zzz*, while the Japanese sound is translated as *bun, bun*. There are several dozen animals speaking through audio files and printed phonetics in well over a dozen languages, searchable by animal or language. By choosing, for example, Greek, Hebrew, or Korean, you will obtain a list of the animals followed by the phonetic sound each makes and a link to the sound file.

 ## AUSTRALIAN ANIMALS `PG`

See also Chapter 2—Australia.

http://ausinternet.com/ettamogah/australiananimals.htm

Etta the koala is anxious to show you around his 20-acre South Wales, Australia, bushland home in the Ettamogah Wildlife Sanctuary. All of his friends, such as the shy kangaroo and the wild dingo, will be there. Simply click on Etta's map and choose which of his friends you'd like to meet. There are also coloring pages, games, and crafts. Or, simply site back and listen to Australian music.

AUSTRALIAN WILDLIFE
See also Chapter 2—Australia.

http://www.effect.net.au/wildcare/index.htm

Wildcare Queanbeyan is a volunteer organization dedicated to the three Rs—rescue, rehabilitation, and release—of sick, injured, and orphaned Australian wildlife. Volunteers will share their stories and photographs of some of the animals that have been in their care, including marsupials, birds, and reptiles. We highly recommend the movie showing how a baby kangaroo, born the size of a jellybean, develops and climbs into its mother's pouch.

BIG CATS

http://dialspace.dial.pipex.com/agarman

Spend some time with the "big cats" of the wild. Leopards, lions, tigers, jaguars, cheetahs, and their lesser known relatives are all accessible via this tour and will share their greatest secrets, such as why their eyes glow in the dark. Travel back in time to see how all of the species are related and how they evolved, dangers of extinction, what's being done to keep them alive, and where the various species may be found. There are also an online glossary and copies of *In the Wild*, an e-zine that will keep your students informed about the latest information and discoveries.

CALIFORNIA LIVING MUSEUM (CALM)   `PG`

http://www.calmzoo.org

CALM is a zoo, botanical garden, and natural history museum that displays over 250 unreleasable animals native to California. Your students will be greeted by Caliente the Badger, who will show them the way to the Herpetelogical Center and the places where some of his fellow residents, such as the San Joaquin kit fox, birds of prey, Whiskers the mountain lion, and the mule deer, can often be found. Caliente is usually anxious to return to his home remodeling project (he's constantly rearranging his burrows), so more in-depth information about zoo residents may be found within *Creature Features*, where students may obtain scientific information including genus and species (Caliente is known as *taxidea taxus*), characteristics, and natural environments. Younger students will want to visit *Kid's Stuff*, which has activities and games, including downloadable mountain lion and raccoon masks to cut out and color, a coyote picture, and a grizzly color-by-number picture that also involves simple subtraction.

CHEETAHS
http://www.cheetahspot.com

Despite the advertising banners that appear on this site, a tour to the *Cheetah Spot* is a worthwhile field trip. Students will be able to look at pictures of live cheetahs (including the rare King Cheetah—only seen in the wild six times) and hear their chirps, purrs, bleats, barks, and growls. There is a lot of fascinating information at this site. Students will learn, for example, how everything in this aerodynamic animal's anatomy, including its teeth, helps it to achieve running speeds of up to 75 miles per hour.

CUB DEN   `PG`
http://www.nature-net.com/bears/cubden.html

This tour is designed "for bears everywhere and for those children who are on their side." Younger students will have the opportunity to view bears in the wild and learn that a cub is able to eat 50 hamburgers and 12 large orders of fries per day. There is a wealth of scientific information for older students. Don Middleton, the proprietor of the *Cub Den,* insists that, "Bears need each child to believe that they can make a difference in the world."

ELEPHANTS   `PG`
http://www.wildheart.com/index.html

Ollie and Ellie Funt will escort your students to the world of their large, very large, family. In addition to information and interesting facts, this elephantine site includes elephant quizzes, sounds, coloring pages, "I love elephant badges," stories and poems, and even a collection of elephant humor. Be sure to try the "elephant walk" with your students. Ollie and Ellie provide the appropriate music on site.

THE FROGGY PAGE   `PG`
http://frog.simplenet.com/froggy

Sandra Loosemore, a research programmer at Yale University, has created *The Froggy Page,* and as soon as you enter her pond, you know you've come to a unique place. "This page contains links to froggy things from various places on the Net for your enjoyment. Ribbet!" By clicking on the word *ribbet,* you will hear an actual frog sound, and if that one croak whets your appetite, you can then choose from a menu of other frog sounds: *blup ka-blurp,* east Texas frog croaks, *peep-peep,* and lots of *greedeeps.* That's just the beginning of the frog information and resources Ms. Loosemore has lovingly compiled. There are mythic frog tales, short stories, and poems; frog clip-art and silly frog images; famous frogs (including the Frog Prince and Kermit); frog songs; and a game of tic-tac-toad. There is also a great deal of serious information, including a link to a site that allows students to perform a complete online virtual frog dissection.

KRATT'S CREATURES   PG
http://www.pbs.org/kratts

Take a behind-the-scenes tour of the PBS television series, *Kratt's Creatures*. Students can travel the world from the jungles and savannas of Africa to the subzero temperatures of Antarctica with Chris and Martin to learn about some of their favorite animals. Simply click on the world map to tell them where you want to go. Multimedia adventures may be found in *Creature Crazy*, and *Creature of the Week* gives students an opportunity to see how much they've learned through an interactive multiple choice quiz.

TURTLE TRAX
http://www.turtles.org

Turtle Trax is devoted to marine turtles and prevention of extinction. Administrators want to let people get to know these amazing creatures and find out why they are threatened and endangered. Younger students may want to stick to the *Kidz Corner* with its more basic information, such as how to build a turtle sundae, stories, and student essays. Although more basic, teachers should be aware that some of the information and photographs may be too graphic for certain children because turtle diseases and accidents are graphically depicted. Photographs and texts are also available for older students.

WOLVES
http://www.wolf.org

The award-winning International Wolf Center focuses on educating the public about wolves and dispelling myths. Wolves, for example, howl at each other, not at the moon. There is an extensive collection of information, wolf images, and telemetry data where classrooms are able to monitor wolf movements through an online map.

ZOOS

Birmingham Zoo
http://www.birminghamzoo.com

The folks at the Birmingham Zoo have been busy adding features to their virtual tour. In addition to the *Flamingo Web Cam* and movies of things like seal lion training sessions and baby camels, students can join in periodic live chats with the zookeeper. If you miss the chat, feel free to e-mail questions. The zookeepers take annual trips to such places as Africa, and are more than willing to have students accompany them. Or board the *Animal Omnibus* and choose from the dozens of animals with links to other resources on the World Wide Web. However, the zoo does not check these pages, so teachers may want to supervise this part of the field trip.

Buffalo Zoological Gardens

http://drew.buffalo.k12.ny.us/drew/tours/zoo/zootours.html

The kids at the Dr. Charles R. Drew Magnet School (grades 4–8) are lucky enough to attend a school located on the grounds of the Buffalo Zoological Gardens. As part of their daily "zoo class," they host this tour of the animals that live at the gardens, including the American bison, animals of the Asian forest, bears, predators, primates, rare and nocturnal creatures, and reptiles. The trip is personalized by brief biographies and photographs of the student writers.

National Zoo

http://natzoo.si.edu

The Smithsonian Institution's National Zoo is the nation's first biopark—a concept that attempts to illustrate the interaction between animals, plants, and human beings by serving as a zoo, natural history museum, and center for scholarly research. If you have the time, one-hour multimedia tours are available, during which zookeepers, curators, and researchers share their stories and knowledge about the plants and animals at the zoo. If not, feel free to tour the many exhibits on your own, including the 17 Web cams that constantly monitor and observe 12 species. Online chats with experts and educational games are also available.

Oregon Zoo

http://www.zooregon.org

The 64-acre Portland, Oregon, zoo is home to almost 1,300 animals of 200 species, and this tour includes photographs and fact sheets for almost all of them. If you arrive early in the morning, you can watch the zookeepers at work. They begin their day by preparing breakfast for all of the zoo's residents and spend a lot of time figuring out how to keep the animals mentally challenged. (It's hard to keep coming up with new smells for the tigers to discover.) There are also a live rhino cam and information about the zoo's efforts to save animals from extinction. If you still want to know more, the zookeeper happily accepts e-mail questions.

CHAPTER 7

SCIENCE AND INDUSTRY

See also Chapter 2—Australia, Chapter 4—Volcanoes and Weather, and 13—4,000 Years of Women in Science, African-Americans in the Sciences, and Tesla, Nikola.

It's one thing to go under the hood of an automobile and quite another to go inside an atom. Your students can see how crayons and chocolate bars are made, or how cells are made. Whether they want to practice cloning or travel inside their brains and organs, we've got a virtual field trip for them. If you're exhausted at the end of the day, relax and tend a garden—in Austria.

INDUSTRY AND INDUSTRIAL ARTS

Automobiles

http://www.innerauto.com/innerauto/htm/auto.html

Everything one might or might not want to know about automobiles can be found at this site. From A.C. compressor drive rings to wheel lugs, there are descriptions, images, trivial facts, and easy-to-understand descriptions of the mechanics of automobiles. This tour is an excellent resource for students, do it yourself mechanics, and anyone who has had to deal with repair garages.

Crayola Factory   PG

http://www.crayola.com

Did you ever wonder how many crayons it would take to reach the moon, or where the word "crayon" originated? The folks who manufacture Crayolas will answer all your students' questions during this tour, while showing them how crayons are manufactured. There are a lot of activities to keep younger students busy, such as interactive stories, crafts, coloring books, and games. Special sections of the tour have been designed for preschoolers, parents, and teachers.

Hershey Foods

PG

http://www.hersheys.com/index.shtml

It's safer than Willie Wonka's. The folks from Hershey will take you on a "chocolate" tour where you will learn how candy bars are made, from the gathering of cacao beans to the final molding process. They'll also tell you about the history of chocolate, dating back to 200 B.C. While you're there, learn how to make a pizza brownie or play a game of Reese's pong.

SCIENCE—ANATOMY

See also Science—Health and Science—Museums and Laboratories—Franklin Institute Science Museum.

Body Quest

http://library.thinkquest.org/10348

This interactive tour of the human body, designed by 11- to 16-year-old students, provides an introduction to various systems and organs and allows your students to delve further into any topic of interest. There are experiments (find out why we have two eyes), quizzes, discussion boards, and virtual models that allow students to rotate, examine, tour, or dissect various systems and organs.

The Brain

http://faculty.washington.edu/chudler/neurok.html

Take your students on a tour of the human brain and spinal cord, hosted by Professor Eric Chudler, a research assistant professor in the Department of Anesthesiology at the University of Washington in Seattle. Chudler has included a long list of activities and games to help students learn about their senses, perceptions, and neurophysiology. He leads grades 3–12 through making models of the brain and neural systems, teaches students how to play synaptic tag outdoors, and even takes them on an Internet neuroscience treasure hunt.

Cells Alive

http://www.cellsalive.com

You may not have a magic school bus, but you can still take your students down into the cells. Photographs, movies, and animations explore a variety of phenomena, from the battle waged between bacteria and white and red blood cells around a splinter to how HIV infiltrates the cells.

Health

http://kidshealth.org

It's off to Philadelphia, where The Nemours Foundation, which operates the Alfred DuPont Hospital for Children, is running a series of seminars that answer questions about kids' bodies ranging from how their muscular systems work to why they throw up. Through animations, quizzes, and activities, kids can see and hear the insides of their bodies as they eat an apple; read interactive journals about kids with diabetes, asthma, and broken bones; learn about every major body system; understand why they burp; and learn what ear wax really is. Check out the healthy recipes while you're there. There are separate sections for kids and teens, each with over a hundred articles and activities. (Teens' questions aren't as much about throwing up and burping as about acne, steroids, alcohol, and sexually transmitted diseases.)

The Respiratory System

http://www.med.virginia.edu/docs/cmc/tutorials/asthma

Asthma is increasing so rapidly among our children that some doctors are calling it an epidemic. Children with asthma, as well as their parents and peers, will want to take a virtual trip to the Children's Medical Center at the University of Virginia, where they can learn all about the condition and the respiratory system through easy-to-understand texts, pictures, movies, and sounds. By clicking on pictures of kids with asthma, students can hear what they feel like when they have an attack, watch a movie showing what normal breathing looks like, and hear normal and abnormal breathing through a stethoscope. There is also a detailed section about available treatments.

SCIENCE—AVIATION AND AEROSPACE
See also Chapter 3.

Aeronautics Learning Laboratory

http://www.allstar.fiu.edu

NASA's ALLSTAR (Aeronautic Learning Laboratory for Science Technology and Research) offers multimedia lessons in the history of aeronautics, aerospace education and careers, and aeronautical principles. Each section of the tour is divided into three grade levels, so you're certain to find materials keyed to your students. There is a special section for teachers, with lesson plans and curriculum correlated to the National Science Standards and the Florida Sunshine State Standards.

National Air & Space Museum—Smithsonian Institution

http://www.nasm.si.edu/NASMhome.html

What better way to tour the Smithsonian's National Air and Space Museum than without crowds? Simply enter the virtual museum, look at the floor plan, and click on the gallery you choose to visit. Tours of the *Enola Gay,* the *Apollo* craft, and World War I and II aircraft are always available. There are also special, changing exhibits, so stop by as often as time allows.

San Diego Aerospace Museum

http://www.aerospacemuseum.org

Take your students on an illustrated tour of the history of aviation, from da Vinci's sketches through space travel. In addition to memorable moments such as the Wright brothers' famous Kitty Hawk flight, World War I and II combat, and jet age fighter and spy planes, students will be able to meet the engineers, pilots, and industrialists instrumental in aerospace history and learn about the process of airplane restoration.

United States Air Force Museum

http://www.wpafb.af.mil/museum

This historical tour of Air Force aviation is provided courtesy of English-, Spanish-, German-, and French-speaking tour guides from Ohio's Wright-Patterson Air Force Base. Tours include pictures of the Huffman Prairie Flying Field where the Wright brothers developed their skills, Century Series Fighters, World War II USAAF and foreign aircraft, the presidential aircraft collection, and the Lockheed Advanced Development Department. (Watch your students to make sure they don't take pictures of anything highly sensitive.) The museum's organization and terminology can be a bit confusing. For example, the *History Gallery* is divided into eras of flight, and although there is interesting information about celebrities such as Clark Gable, Jimmy Stewart, Joe Louis, and Ronald Regan, it's difficult to find if you don't know they served in the military.

SCIENCE—BIOLOGY AND BOTANY   PG

Cool Science for Curious Kids

http://www.hhmi.org/coolscience/

The Howard Hughes Medical Institute invites your students on an interactive biological exploration. First, scientists will train your students to look very closely at ordinary things and have them fill out a downloadable observation checklist. Then it's off to some biological and botanical classification exercises. By the end of the day, students will know why monkeys are like moose and why butterflies look nothing at all like caterpillars. This is a fairly basic site, appropriate for primary grades.

Mendel Web

http://www.netspace.org/MendelWeb

Gregor Mendel would be amazed by the technological applications of his famous 1865 work, "Experiments in Plant Hybridization." The modern version of Mendel's original paper, available in both German and English, has been annotated by students around the world, and the hosts have provided glossaries, images, interactive statistical calculations, and audiovisual materials. Visitors will gain an excellent understanding of the origins of genetics, introductory data analysis, and plant science.

Microbiology—Tour 1
http://www.microbe.org

Sam Sleuth (who has been trained by the American Society for Microbiology) will guide your elementary school students through the world of microbiology. As they follow Sam to the Himalayas and landfills and into common colds, they'll learn that microbes aren't just nasty germs—some are essential to our life. Students whose interests are "germinated" can learn all about careers in the field of microbiology.

Microbiology—Tour 2
http://www.pfizer.com/rd/microbes

The folks at Pfizer, Inc., tell us that microbes are not trying to make anyone sick—they're just trying to survive. Take this tour for an excellent overall view of the world of viruses, bacteria, protozoa, and fungi. Don't miss the *Fun Zone,* where your students can join Pfizer scientists in their laboratories (they'll be happy to let you use their electron microscopes) or step into their time machine and explore the evolution of these fascinating organisms. Students can go as far back as 1347, where they'll learn about the bubonic plague (they'll gain a new outlook on the song "Ring Around the Rosie") and as far forward as 1969 to discover the role of microorganisms in the *Apollo II* space mission.

Virtual Cell
http://www.life.uiuc.edu/plantbio/cell

If your budget precludes the purchase of high-tech equipment, pay a visit to this site and watch as Metez Lexa, from the University of Illinois at Chicago, turns your computer into a microscope. Students can examine a virtual reproduction of a single plant cell by dissecting, focusing, and turning in various directions. Animations and other images and texts explain the cell's structure and functions. Lexa cautions your students to "beware of flying chloroplasts."

Virtual Garden
http://www.usc.edu/dept/garden

Perhaps your class would like to explore and help take care of a garden, along with other people from around the world. An actual garden has been set up, tended by a robotic arm that visitors are able to control from their own computers. Although it is possible to visit the "telegarden" as either a guest on a guided tour or a member (free of charge), only members can actually control the robotic arm.

SCIENCE—BIOTECHNOLOGY AND CLONING

Conceiving a Clone

http://library.advanced.org/24355/home.html

Don your laboratory coats and head to the lab, where students can perform a simulated cloning. Before you leave, you may want to read the pros and cons of the process, provided on site. There is also a "cloning timeline," covering the history of genetics, beginning in 1885 with August Weismann's theory. Animations including the first cloned farm animal, chain reactions, and the recombinant DNA process are certain to hold the interest of any student.

SCIENCE—CHEMISTRY

Learning Matters of Chemistry

http://www.knowledgebydesign.com/tlmc/tlmc.html

Dr. Yue-Ling Wong has developed this interactive chemistry site with tutorials, animations, movies, and practice exercises. Students will love the Tetris-style periodic table game, online graphing pad, and molecular weight calculator. The graphics and other materials make concepts such as molecular modeling, atomic orbitals, and the Bohr model easy to understand and fun to learn.

Molecules

http://www.iumsc.indiana.edu/common/common.html

Take your students to Indiana University's multimedia tour of the structure of common and uncommon molecules and crystals. Using x-ray crystallography, students will learn about a variety of molecules. Be sure to check the *Weird and Neat Stuff* like the buckyball.

SCIENCE—EARTH AND ENVIRONMENTAL

Carolina Coastal Science

http://www.ncsu.edu/coast

North Carolina's Shell Island resort is in trouble. Due to natural forces, a major inlet is shifting, and Dr. Alec M. Bodzin, Assistant Professor of Science Education at Lehigh University, is asking for your students' help in deciding what can be done. Taking various roles such as shareholders, homeowners, and local business owners, students will use videos, graphics, and texts to help them make decisions. If that's too much to handle, they can decide whether to move the historic Cape Hatteras lighthouse, which is on an eroding spit of land. This interactive inquiry-based science tour is based on the National Science Education Standards, and Dr. Bodzin believes that although it is designed for elementary and middle school environmental science, the tour is also suitable for upper secondary science students. The issues incorporate science with social studies, geography, language, and media studies. Teaching suggestions and detailed curriculum guides are provided.

Dodoland

PG

http://www.swifty.com/azatlan

This site, sponsored by numerous nonprofit organizations, is dedicated to helping small children develop a respect and appreciation for our planet, the environment, and each other. The concept of *Dodoland* as a fun place where children learn respect for all living things began as a book about 20 years ago in Los Angeles, became a play in New York City, and has since spawned workshops in creative writing, art, music, dance, and drama. A typical "issue" of *Dodoland* begins on giant Flower Island, where kids have a choice of writing, learning environmentally oriented games, or, in one wonderfully imaginative segment, clicking on a photo of a rainbow and finding themselves right near the gaping jaws of a hippo. They can then click inside the hippo's yawning mouth and end up just outside the ancient city of Machu Picchu, covered with clouds. In another segment, kids send an e-mail message expressing their wish for Earth, and they can read what other kids have submitted. (One child wrote, "Please help the Earth. It's crying out to you like the eagle child.")

The Ozone Hole

http://www.atm.ch.cam.ac.uk/tour

The Centre for Atmospheric Science at the University of Cambridge provides this tour of the ozone hole from its first initial discovery in 1970 to current research. Through movies, animations, and narratives, students will watch the ozone hole develop, find out how it began and what efforts are being made to repair it, and learn about the science of polar meteorology and how measurements and research are conducted. The somewhat technical tour is geared toward students in upper grades.

SCIENCE—FORENSICS

http://library.advanced.org/17049/gather

Susie Van Konkel is missing, and your students, using tools of forensic science, have to find her. As they sleuth, they'll learn about the many applications of and careers in forensic science, from medical testing to crime investigation.

SCIENCE—GENERAL

Beakman's Place

http://www.beakman.com

Visit the popular television science show, *Beakman's Place*, to learn why your feet smell or why your stomach doesn't disintegrate when it secretes hydrochloric acid. Beakman tells us that "a question is a powerful thing," and he is willing to answer just about anything one might want to know. Experiments and games clarify many of his answers to questions such as, "Which way is up?" We know your students will be interested when Beakman shows them how to make "mucus and boogers" with the same ingredients that your body uses (protein and sugars), what happens to your lungs when you smoke, and where ear wax comes from (there's even a close-up view).

Mad Scientist Network

http://www.madsci.org

Did you ever wonder how many calories the brain can burn up, how quicksand actually works, or why your grandfather eventually stops growing? Wonder no more. A group of graduate and medical students at Washington University in St. Louis has established the *Mad Scientist Network*, a "cranial collective" of over 200 scientists from around the world in over 23 fields of science who will answer any question. Simply e-mail your question, and one of the scientists will respond. Questions and answers are topically archived on site; etiquette dictates that you first read the archives to make sure your question has not already been answered. The archives are also searchable by grade level, so students can see what their world-wide peers have been wondering about.

Science Odyssey

http://www.pbs.org/wgbh/aso/index.html

Take a journey through 100 years of science with the folks at PBS, where your students will acquire some much-needed perspective—and have fun too. They'll learn that in 1900, the Earth was considered 50 million years old; today, we think it's 4,500 million years old. In 1900, doctors could do little more than comfort patients and keep them clean. Separate timelines take your students on a 100-year tour of medicine, human behavior, physics, technology, and evolution. Online comic books present Rachel Carson's *Silent Spring*, the story of Jonas Salk's polio vaccine, and the discoveries of pulsars and AIDS. Play, "What's My Theory?" against a panel of Einsteins or Freuds by asking them questions and, from their answers, trying to separate the real Einstein or Freud from the imposters. When students have learned enough, they can try their own hand at moving on-screen mountains and continents, probing a brain, or watching household items appear and disappear as they move around in time. Teachers will want to check out the resource section for additional classroom materials. Although some materials are keyed to the program's broadcasts of a few years ago, many resources are available on site.

The Why Files

http://whyfiles.news.wisc.edu

Take your class to *The Why Files* for the inside scoop behind science news. This National Institute for Science Education project adds new features twice a month, and files are maintained from prior features. Whether it's outer space, cellular biology, or the statistics of political polling, here's where to learn the science behind the news. Past issues addressed the relationship between eyesight and diet, spinal cord injuries, life on Mars, the hazards of space travel, and nicotine addiction. Be sure to check the latest *Cool Science Image.*

SCIENCE—GEOLOGY, GEMS, AND MINERALS

http://www.bsu.edu/teachers/academy/gems/index.html

This tour to the Janet Annenberg Hooker Hall of Geology, Gems, and Minerals at the Smithsonian's Museum of Natural History is designed for students in grades 7–12. Scientists and researchers not only cover the beauty, worth, and cultural aspects of gems and minerals but also relate the substances to our planet and bodies. Be sure to check the tour's *Activities* section, developed in conjunction with the Stark County, Ohio, Educational Service Center. Each activity is listed with its corresponding National Science Education Standard(s) and covers sampling techniques, minerals in the human body and the home, and mineral diversity. Several of the activities incorporate other curricular areas such as mathematics and English.

SCIENCE—HEALTH—DRUG AND ALCOHOL ADDICTION

See also Science—Anatomy.

http://www.pbs.org/closetohome/home.html

Marla worries that people will not take her seriously because of her looks. Although she is going away to college in the fall, she still worries about being trapped in her home town forever. Wilson Tucker, on the other hand, fears boredom and "straights," who laugh at him when he zones out; no wonder his favorite subject is lunch. Beau is struggling through his first year of sobriety. These teens are all part of *Overboard,* an interactive comic book dealing with addiction. The 13-issue book was designed to accompany a PBS Bill Moyers report on addiction. Students read real-life stories of those struggling with the problem, take part in on-line discussions, and view some of the controversial debates taking place between various experts.

SCIENCE—MATERIALS
http://www.lbl.gov/MicroWorlds

This interactive tour of the Lawrence Berkeley National Laboratory's Advanced Light Source is geared toward high school students. Scientists will show students how the Advanced Light Source machine works, what polymers are and why they are useful, how infinitesimal quantities of trace elements can change a material, how scientists make machines that can fit through the eye of a needle, and how materials science helps in understanding environmental problems. Problems are posed, with clues that encourage inquiry-based learning. For example, the section on selenium poses the question of how wetlands may have become contaminated with selenium and how they can be cleaned up. In Clue #1, students are told about selenium's properties and asked what uses they can think of for this material. Subsequent clues guide them along the problem and solution trail.

SCIENCE—MICROSCOPY

The Microscopic World
http://www.pbrc.hawaii.edu/kunkel

Delving into the microscopic world with Dennis Kunkel, Ph.D., from the University of Hawaii, is a fascinating experience. Kunkel has provided photomicrographs taken with light and electron microscopes. We suggest you begin your tour of this miniature world by reading the brief introductory materials provided (*About Microscopy*). We especially liked the *Most Wanted Bugs* section, with "mug shots" and "rap sheets." You won't believe how different the friendly ladybug (aka Spot) looks under a microscope.

Nanoworld
http://www.uq.oz.au/nanoworld/nanohome.html

The Centre for Microscopes and Microanalysis at the University of Queensland will take you on a tour of the microscopic world. The center is dedicated to the understanding of the structure and composition of all atomic, molecular, cellular, and macromolecular scales. Students will be able to see the world from a different perspective while they tour blood cells, bone marrow, and other material structures. The magnified mosquito is on a par with any of the horror movies today's students seem to love so much—only it is far more informative and educational. The *Virtual Electronic Microscope* is an interactive on-site tool through which students can view the Queensland fruit fly and other exhibits. There is also an extensive section describing how microscopes are used in the manufacture of circuits.

SCIENCE—MUSEUMS AND LABORATORIES

Argonne National Laboratories

http://www.anl.gov

It's off to Chicago and Idaho Falls, where scientists working at America's first national laboratory and one of the Department of Energy's largest research centers will answer your students' questions. (They've already answered over 15,000 questions from students around the world, all of which are archived on site.) Topics include astronomy, biology, chemistry, engineering, the environment, general science, math, physics, and technology. Be sure to check the *Gee Whiz* portion of the tour, where students can work along with scientists as they view various operations in microscope rooms and analyze data being recorded by various constantly operating detector systems. They'll even be allowed access to the rooms where the movie *Chain Reaction* was filmed. High school teachers should be certain to see how their students can enter the laboratory's annual Rube Goldberg contest.

Australian National Science and Technology Museum

http://www.questacon.edu.au/body_planning_a_visit.html

Take your class "down under" to this three-dimensional science museum for students of all ages. We suggest you begin your tour by checking out the teachers' section. Every year, the museum has an Internet project that connects students around the world, and here's where you'll find the information. This is also a good place to begin planning your tour: There's so much going on that you'll need to get organized ahead of time. Past exhibits have included an on-screen light harp (clicking on different colors produces different tones), a trip into the three-dimensional past where students can compare their speed against dinosaurs, and exhibits on optical illusions and Tasmanian tigers. There are always interactive puzzles and quizzes.

Boston Museum of Science

http://www.mos.org/home.html

The Boston Museum of Science takes your students from the farthest reaches of outer space, where they'll search for signs of life, to Antarctica. Almost a dozen trips challenge your students to think about how they communicate nonverbally, witness the awesome power and myriad uses of electricity, explore Mt. Everest and the oceans, and go on an archaeological dig underneath Boston. We especially enjoyed the nonverbal communication tour, where students study collages drawn by others and try to guess the artists' ages.

Chicago Academy of Sciences

http://www.chias.org

Elementary school students and teachers are invited to the Chicago Academy of Science. Be sure to visit the *Chaos Club,* where students are welcome to watch Web movies covering a variety of topics. We recommend going on the *Strange Case of the Mystery Rock* tour. After making initial observations of the strange rock in an online journal, students are provided with tools and choose whether to study it further with a tweezers, hammer, or toothpick. Eventually students discover, hopefully on their own, that the rock is actually a—well, we don't want to ruin the surprise. Others may prefer to visit the online dioramas at the *Peggy Notebaert Nature Museum.* Originally created in 1914, the works depict the dunes and prairies of the Chicago region as they appeared in 1880. The Academy has thoughtfully created a special area for teachers where they are able to obtain lesson plans and other classroom activities.

Children's Museum of Indianapolis

http://www.childrensmuseum.org

The folks at the Children's Museum of Indianapolis have provided a special wing just for your students. Pay a visit to *Fun On Line* and get ready for a variety of educational, interactive experiences. In the past, artist John Payne showed how to create kinetosaurs, moving dinosaur sculptures that integrate science and art. With movies and text, students learned how to make papier mâché dinosaurs and dinosaur wire sculptures and mobiles. A dinosaur database helped them construct accurate models and even imagine their own. At *Cosmic Quest,* students figured out how to design a space station by matching wits with top engineers from NASA and the Russian Space Agency. (If the exhibit is still online, watch the looks on your students' faces when they lift off from Earth.) Exhibits at the museum are constantly being added, so we suggest you check frequently. We can't predict what you'll find, but we guarantee it will be inquiry-based, fun, and very interesting.

Field Museum of Natural History

http://www.fmnh.org

Pay a visit to the Field Museum of Natural History on Chicago's lakefront and check the latest online exhibits, including Sue, the largest tyrannosaurus rex skeleton ever found. The core collections center around biology and anthropology and include the extensive exhibit *Life Over Time,* which uses paintings, vivid texts, activities, games, and animated movies that allow students to examine life from the beginning of time through the dinosaur period and into the Neanderthal and Piltdown eras. Excerpts from the teacher's guide to the exhibit are included with pre- and post-tour classroom lesson plans. Others may prefer to see what life in the soil is like when you are only one-half inch tall. (Don't worry, you are able to transmogrify first, so you can get used to your new size.) After living among the many creatures of the soil, you might want to rise above ground and tour the *Butterfly Net,* an extensive moth and butterfly collection. When we last checked, there was also an exhibit on the maneless, man-eating lions of Tsovo, Kenya. And, if your timing is right, the museum's music vault may be open and students will be allowed to play one of the instruments, such as the Javanese gamelon, using digital technology.

Franklin Institute Science Museum

http://sln.fi.edu

Folks from the Franklin Institute Science Museum want to let you know that their doors are always open to you and your students. In addition to permanent exhibits such as *The Heart: An Online Exploration* and the life and works of Ben Franklin, there are rotating monthly exhibits covering a variety of science topics. Last time we checked, we were able to wander through the *Inquiry Attic* and learn about nineteenth-century patent models, historical celestial globes, Maillardet's mechanical drawing machine, Franklin's glass armonica (his greatest personal satisfaction), bicycle technology, and the Wright brothers' wind tunnel and flight notebooks. Teachers will be interested in the changing featured units of study and classroom activities.

Invention Dimension

http://web.mit.edu/invent

Invention Dimension, hosted by the Massachusetts Institute of Technology, features a different American inventor each week. Information includes a biographical sketch covering the inventor's accomplishments and the impact of the invention on society. Just about anyone you would want to meet can be found in the archives, from Ben Franklin to Steve Wozniak of Apple Computer. Students inspired to create their own inventions should check the *Inventor's Handbook*, a step-by-step guide to the invention and patent processes.

Natural History Museum of London

http://www.nhm.ac.uk

Students of all ages can spend weeks at London's Natural History Museum, which hosts a number of interactive exhibits relating to the natural and physical world. This tour is ideal for inquiry-based learning, with virtual endeavors, reality, and data files. The *Earth Lab Database*, for example, allows students to investigate the fossils, minerals, and rocks of the United Kingdom by selecting various classifications, ages, groups, elements, and properties. *Quest* is an exploratory simulation where students are able to select a number of natural objects to explore, all of which can be viewed from various angles, enlarged, weighed, measured, felt, observed under ultraviolet lighting, etc. If students want to know more, scientists are available online to answer questions. Students are asked to make scientific notes, which are archived on site, allowing them to compare their observations with those made by other students around the world. There is also a *Science Casebook* where one can take the role of a museum scientist and seek answers to such questions as whether humans will be able to re-create dinosaurs.

National Museum of Natural History—Smithsonian Institution

http://www.mnh.si.edu

For over a century, the Smithsonian Institution's National Museum of Natural History has been assembling collections of natural and cultural developments, and your students are invited to see them. The best way to tour this extensive site, with its frequently changing online exhibits, is to choose *Research and Collections*, where information is filed by Anthropology, Biology, Entomology, Invertebrate Zoology, Mineral Sciences, Paleobiology, and Vertebrate Zoology. Simply click on the department of interest to keep apprised of the current online exhibits, as well as a general background on the specific field of science.

Ontario Science Centre

http://www.osc.on.ca

The folks at the Ontario Science Centre offer several interactive multimedia exhibits to allow your students to "have some fun with their grey matter." Students can use the center's "computer crayons" to see how they work by taking colors away from white paper, learn about the art of camouflage, feel the confusion of the *Stroop Effect,* and even experience *The Marvelous Exploding Zit.* Tours are available in both French and English.

Perpetual Motion Collection

http://manor.york.ac.uk/htdocs/perpetual/perpetual.html

Richard G. Clegg of the United Kingdom invites you to view his collection of perpetual motion machines, including the underwater swimming donut. Each machine comes with a diagram and an explanation of how it works. There's also an explanation of how each machine does not work—because, as everyone knows, there is no such thing as perpetual motion.

Royal British Columbia Museum

http://rbcm1.rbcm.gov.bc.ca/index_rc.html

The *Special Collections* at Victoria's Royal British Columbia Museum focus on the region's ecology and endangered species. Tours, available in either English or French, provide photographs and information about plants and animals in the Thompson-Okanagan region and audio recordings of local birds.

San Diego Natural History Museum

http://www.sdnhm.org/home.html

There's something for just about everybody at San Diego, California's, Natural History Museum. We suggest you begin your tour at the *Kid's Habitat*, where you can don your pith helmet and travel back to the Mesozoic era for a dinosaur dig. Guides will show you how to find fossils while you ponder the theories of meteors and mass extinction. Or, roll up your sleeves and hang around with the museum's geologists, who will show you how to identify minerals—you'll be able to start your own collection or grow your own crystals. If you prefer the water, stop in at the *Shark School* for a deep sea dive with marine biologists. Others may prefer to stay indoors and play games such as *Name That Reptile* (you'll find that there's a lot more to scientific names than you might think) or help museum personnel care for the resident insects. Be sure to check the museum's *Field Guide*, an exploration of the terrain, climate, and living things of southern California, the Baja Peninsula, and surrounding waters and islands.

San Francisco Exploratorium

http://www.exploratorium.edu

The *San Francisco Exploratorium* is one of the oldest Internet hands-on museums and a perennial favorite of teachers. Tours are conducted in English, Spanish, French, and Italian. The topics of online exhibits cover a wide range and have included the science of vocal cords (what happens when you give someone "the raspberry") the science of baseball, mutant fruit flies, and optical illusions (images that seem to fade, shimmer, or change colors the longer you stare at them). This extensive site has an organization that often seems serendipitous, so leave yourself time to explore. Some of the projects, such as a real-time online video conference with seismic scientists, require considerable advance planning. The *Exploratorium* also presents projects and experiments that have been developed by teachers, such as building a fog chamber and studying the Doppler effect. There is also an online book that students are welcome to take home to further their studies. They can learn how to make their own cartoons using "flipsticks," how to build a geodesic dome out of gumdrops, and become aircraft designers with "spinning blimps."

Science Museum of London

http://www.nmsi.ac.uk/welcome.html

There's always something of interest at the Science Museum of London. *Hands on Science* has interactive exhibits such as virtual experiments that will allow students to discover how their vision and brains work and interact. Others may prefer to watch the movies that explain the contribution that artists made to the engineering of the Renaissance. Be sure to stop by the *Launch Pad,* where students can build an arch bridge, learn about forces and motion, or find out about sound waves through an interactive mini-synthesizer.

Yuckiest Site on the Internet

http://www.yucky.com

This site is proudly proclaimed to be "The Yuckiest Site on the Internet" because it focuses on scientific topics of gross interest, such as "gross body sounds" of gurgling stomachs or borborygmus—food being pushed through the intestines. Students can learn about barfing, belching, and blackheads, and naturally, there's a cockroach exhibit. Mary Appelhof, aka The Worm Woman, tells your students how and why she raises worms, and what inspired her to do it. We recommend the video of Mary inside her worm box for after lunch. Which brings us to the many, actually edible recipes for things such as eyeball eggs and worms in the mud (made with chocolate pudding, gummy worms, and graham crackers). Surely you'll want to go on some of the activities such as the nauseating nature hunt. Not everything is yucky. The dozens of experiments and activities include writing with invisible ink (lemon juice) and rubbing your closed eyes in the dark and watching subsequent bursts and patterns of light. (The explanation: Rubbing your eyes stimulates your brain and optic nerves.)

SCIENCE—OPTICAL ILLUSIONS

http://www.illusionworks.com

Can we really be certain of what we are seeing? Can perception differ from reality? Visit the *Optical Illusion Collection* and find out the answers to these questions. Administrators claim this is the most comprehensive collection on the World Wide Web, with pictographic and three-dimensional distortions, stereographic illusions, interactive demonstrations and puzzles, and color contrast effects. Choose either the advanced or introductory sections, which differ in the intricacy of the illusions and complexity of the explanations.

http://www.grand-illusions.com

Administrators of this site promise "optical illusions, scientific toys, and even a little magic." This tour will allow your students to discover some of the secrets of the magic mirror, and even the moon—one of the most famous optical illusions. Richard Gregory, emeritus professor of neuropsychology at the University of Bristol, presents *An Introduction to Seeing,* and Tim Rowlett, who collects extraordinary toys and novelties, gadgets, inventions, and optical and topological devices, will open up some of his 95 suitcases with 7,000 toys for you. He'll explain how some of these unusual toys—such as the super magnet, the levitron, the Chinese singing fountain, and the fountain pen without a center—work. There are also interesting articles and stories such as *The Strange Story of Napoleon's Wallpaper.*

http://www.sandlotscience.com/

Explore over 75 optical illusions, including "impossible" objects, distortions that "mock common sense and taunt reason," contrast and color, typography, ambiguous illusions with "multiple personalities," after effects, camouflage, and morie patterns. There are games and puzzles, as well as the *Story of Optical Illusions*, which we're told is as old as history itself.

SCIENCE—PALEONTOLOGY

Paleontology Without Walls

http://www.ucmp.berkeley.edu/exhibit/exhibits.html

This tour, sponsored by the University of California at Berkeley, allows students to explore the science of paleontology through the fields of phylogeny, geologic time, and evolutionary theories. What better man to tour the discovery and reconstruction of the dilophosauras with than Sam Welles, the man who actually discovered it. You can also check out dinosaurs, current research, Sulawesi coelacanths (discovered by University of Berkeley researchers), the great white shark, sabertooths, and vertebrate flight. Personnel will also take your students on a tour of the Paleontological Institute of Russia to learn about the dinosaurs of Mongolia and the giant mammals of the tertiary era. The exhibit also includes biographies of over a dozen scientists, from Aristotle and da Vinci to Paley and Wegener, many of their works, and a glossary.

SCIENCE—PHYSICS

ABCs of Nuclear Science

http://www.lbl.gov/abc

Have you ever eaten radioactive food? You might be surprised. Find out about radioactivity and radiation safety; antimatter; nuclear structure; reactions; cosmic rays; and alpha, beta, and gamma decay from the folks at the Lawrence Berkeley National Laboratory. The *ABCs of Nuclear Science* covers such topics as the difference between fission and fusion, the structure of the atomic nucleus, and how elements on Earth were produced. High school teachers and students can find simple experiments such as "Alpha Please Leave Home" or "Stop that Gamma," which can be conducted with inexpensive equipment. Nuclear scientists are available via e-mail to answer your questions.

Aerodynamics in Sports Technology

http://muttley.ucdavis.edu/Tennis

This joint effort between NASA's Learning Technologies Project and Cislunar Aerospace, Inc., uses tennis to teach various concepts of industrial aerodynamics, physics, and math. The techniques of some of the top tennis players in the world are being recorded to gather data on how a tennis ball moves, its speed and spin, what happens when it hits the court, how it moves in the air, and how various strokes generate flight. The project, geared toward grades K–12, makes use of new generation high-speed digital cameras and includes suggested experiments. There will also be live video conferences over the Internet, chats with investigators, and the ability to conduct your own research. Be sure to read the instructions on how your class can take part in the research and learn more about air pressure; density; velocity; ball physics; and the forces of weight, lift, thrust, drag, and the Magnus Effect.

Stanford Linear Accelerator Center

http://www2.slac.stanford.edu/vvc/home.html

The scientists at the Stanford Linear Accelerator Center and Synchrotron Radiation Laboratory have developed this virtual tour especially for teachers and students. Work carried out at the center has earned three Nobel prizes, and now students can delve as deeply into the basic principles of physics as they desire. Tours include the workings of the linear accelerator and particle detectors, examples of electron beams and synchrotron x-rays, and current and planned experiments and research. It's not just about theory—students will also learn about some of the practical applications of physics, such as the development of anti-viral drugs.

Stephen Hawking

http://www.wnet.org/archive/hawking/html/home.html

Stephen Hawking is noted for, among other accomplishments, his ability to make complex physics understandable to the layperson. Despite having spent much of his life confined to a wheel chair with Lou Gehrig's disease, Hawking is the Lucasian Professor of Mathematics at Cambridge, a post once held by Isaac Newton. His physics book, *A Brief History of Time*, was on the *London Sunday Times* bestseller list for four years, the longest run of any book in history. We suggest you begin your tour in the *Strange Stuff Explained* area, where Mr. Hawking makes complex concepts, from antimatter to the Uncertainty Principle, "a little less so." We learned, for example, how time can be imaginary. *Cosmological Stars* recognizes major contributions to the field of cosmology, from Eratosthenes, known as the man who first measured the world, to Marie Curie—the first to coin the term radioactivity—and those who may not be as well known, such as Paul Dirac, one of the pioneers of quantum mechanics. We were surprised to learn that Albert Einstein won the Nobel Prize for his description of the photoelectric effect, in which electrons are emitted when light falls on certain metals, rather than for his theory of relativity. Be sure to check the on-site teacher's guide with vocabulary and activities.

SCIENCE—TECHNOLOGY

Lucent Technologies/Bell Labs

http://www.lucent.com/ideas

Scientists of the past and present welcome your students to their laboratories. People who have made breakthroughs in science will explain how discoveries are made and keep your students apprised of the latest technological advances. Be sure to visit the *Heritage Center* while you're there. During our trip we were able to learn about the transistor through animations and text covering its first commercial application in 1950 to today's high-tech microprocessors. It's not often that you have the opportunity to learn science directly from its inventors—in this case the 1956 Nobel Prize-winning team of John Bardeen, Walter Brattain, and William Shockery.

CHAPTER 8

MATHEMATICS AND LOGIC

Now you can cover the history of mathematics and logic, from Aristotle and the abacus to computer-generated fractal art. Play mind games, enter contests, and learn from the world's leading mathematicians and educational theorists. Let your students ask questions of experts and match wits with their peers around the world.

THE CALCULATOR MUSEUM
http://www.hpmuseum.org

Dave Hicks, who works for Intel, invites you to visit his Hewlett-Packard Calculator Museum (which is not affiliated with the corporation of the same name). In an act of hubris, the history of calculators is divided into two periods, 1614–1968 (or pre-Hewlett-Packard) and 1968–present. Your students will probably be more interested in—or confounded by—the first period, which features slide rules and other primitive contraptions, such as bulky adding machines from the 1940s and 1950s.

CALCULUS

Calculus Graphics Gallery
http://www.math.psu.edu/dna/graphics.html

Take your students to the technology classroom at Pennsylvania State University to see this collection of graphical demonstrations developed for first-year calculus students. Through the use of images, computer animation, online worksheets, and other resources, students will learn to compute the volume of water in a tipped glass, to understand and predict how a ball bounces, and to figure out other basic calculus problems such as Archimedes's calculation of pi, secants and tangents, and the intersection of two cylinders.

Online Tutorial

http://archives.math.utk.edu/visual.calculus

This online tutorial was designed by Larry Husch of the Mathematics Department at the University of Tennessee at Knoxville. An excellent source for those who need a little more help in calculus or want to advance to more complicated topics, the site uses computer graphics and interactive modules to cover pre-calculus, derivatives, differentiation, and integration. Students will find detailed instructions for the use of the TI-85 and TI-86 graphing calculators, interactive quizzes, and drill problems.

COMPUTER MUSEUM

http://www.obsoletecomputermuseum.org

Tom Carlson invites your students to his museum of obsolete personal computers, and his personality is as entertaining as his pictures and descriptions of computers. Don't worry about the nude picture of himself that he promises—he's a jokester.

CONTESTS

Elementary Brain Teasers

http://www.olemiss.edu/mathed/brain/

Casio Company and the University of Mississippi challenge your elementary school students with a new math and/or logic problem every two weeks. Students are asked, for example, to figure out how many guests at a Super Bowl party ate chips, if 12 people were invited, one-third attended, one-half ate wings, and four-sixths ate chips. Winners' names are posted on site.

Middle School Madness

http://www.olemiss.edu/mathed/middle

Middle School Madness is sponsored by the Casio Company and the University of Mississippi's Math Education Program. Every two weeks, students are challenged with a new math problem and an online calculator is provided to help them solve it. By the time we were able to figure out the greatest attainable number when a two-digit number is divided by the sum of its digits, the winners had already been posted on the site. There are also contests for algebra and geometry students.

High School Challenge

http://www.olemiss.edu/mathed/contest/

If your salary was reduced by "P" percent, what percentage would it have to be increased to restore your original salary? Casio Company and the University of Mississippi challenge your high school students with a new math and/or logic problem every two weeks. Appropriate online calculators are provided, and winners' names are posted on site.

COOL MATH

http://www.coolmath4kids.com

A mathematics instructor at a California Community College has developed this *Amusement Park of Mathematics* for students of all ages. Children as young as three will find something of interest, from problems to logic puzzles and games. Our favorite portion of the site is the calculator section, with dozens of machines that convert decimals to binaries, compute the circumference and arc of circles, calculate roman numerals, test prime numbers, and even figure one's age in dog years.

FRACTAL ART

Carlson's Fractal Gallery

http://sprott.physics.wisc.edu/carlson.htm

A tour of *Carlson's Fractal Gallery* will allow your students to see dozens of images, with explanations and the formulas from which they were created. If you can understand the explanations, then you probably already know what fractal art is. If you can't understand, just relax and enjoy the art.

Don Archer's Fractal Art Gallery

http://www.donarcher.com

Don Archer's Fractal Art Gallery has dozens of vivid images of his work, including fractal zoos (both real and imaginary), cameras, gardens, and fault lines. Mr. Archer's prints have been exhibited in several shows, and his work is included in the collection of Ball State University's Art Museum in Muncie, Indiana. An interesting feature of this tour is the *U-Draw Fractal,* where Mr. Archer will create a fractal from random numbers and functions provided by your students. The results will appear on site.

The Fractal Microscope

http://www.ncsa.uiuc.edu/edu/fractal

The Fractal Microscope is an interactive tool, designed by the Education Group at the National Center for Supercomputing Applications, for the exploration of the Mandlebrot set and other fractal patterns. This display is accompanied by explanations of how to use fractal art in the K–12 classroom. Such topics as scientific notation, the coordinates of systems and graphing, number systems, convergence, and divergence are covered. In their words, "fractal geometry mixes art with mathematics to demonstrate that equations are more than just a collection of numbers. Using fractal geometry, students can visually model much of what they see in nature, such as coastlines and mountains."

GEOMETRY CENTER
http://www.geom.umn.edu

The *Geometry Center* is a joint collaboration between the National Science Foundation and the University of Minnesota's Technology Center. Through the use of the Internet, this partnership has succeeded in making the study of geometry interesting, practical, and easy to understand. Of particular interest is the *Interactive Geometry Gallery*, in which students are able to participate in many hands-on activities. For example, the *Web Pisces* allows the implicit computation of defined curves on a plane, and the *Build a Rainbow Gallery* answers common questions about this natural phenomenon by examining a mathematical model of light passing through a water droplet.

HISTORY OF MATHEMATICS ARCHIVE
http://www-history.mcs.st-and.ac.uk/history

St. Andrews University in Scotland has accumulated a collection of over 1,000 mathematics-related biographies and articles and extensive data on over 50 mathematical curves. Click on any item in the index to see the curve's equation, history, and some of its associated curves. There are a variety of choices, from "Asteroid" to "Watts," the curve named after the inventor of the steam engine.

LOS ALAMOS NATIONAL LABORATORY'S MEGA MATH
http://www.c3.lanl.gov/mega-math

The intention of this trip is to bring unusual and important math ideas and concepts to schools. Several areas of mathematics are covered, and each section includes activities, vocabulary, background information, ideas, and key concepts. *The Most Colorful Math of All* shows that coloring is really a mathematical rather than an artistic concept and that it has multimillion-dollar industrial applications. Among other materials, this section presents a problem that has been studied for over 100 years. Some versions of the problem are easy to solve, whereas others could have only been solved with the advent of computers. The basic problem is, "How many colors do you need?" Students answer this question through a range of activities, beginning with figuring out how to use as few colors as possible when placing countries on a map, through proofs of the four-color theorem. *Untangling the Mystery of Knots* has students make and verify observations about knots to show how the study is of interest to theoretical physicists and molecular biologists. *Algorithms and Ice Cream for All* poses the problem of where to put an ice cream stand in a town so that no one person has to go too far for a treat. *Machines That Eat Your Words* deals with a finite-state machine, an imaginary device used to design and study systems that recognize and identify patterns. Students use an ongoing interactive story in *Welcome to Hotel Infinity*, and *Games on Graphs* explores graph theory and shows how graphs are used in computer network design, urban planning, molecular biology, finding the best way to route and schedule airplanes, and even in inventing a secret code. *Just a Usual Day at Unusual School* has students perform various plays that present mathematical problems and concepts. For example, in the *Unusual School* one student always lies while the rest always tell the truth. How do you find out who's lying?

PAVILION OF POLYHEDREALITY
http://www.georgehart.com/pavilion.html

This exhibit is devoted to "practical polyhedra." Students can view real-world examples of this geometric shape while listening to "choreographed" music. Exhibits include *Nailbangers Nightmare* (a simple project for weekend carpenters) and various polyhedra constructed of paper, paper clips, and even apples and oranges. Students will be interested in the 60 forks arranged along the edges of a rhombic triacontahedron. After viewing the exhibits, take your students to the on-site library, where there are 850 polyhedra, explanations of varying levels of difficulty, and suggested projects and quizzes.

WORD PROBLEMS
http://www.mathstories.com

Try some of the word problems at this site to improve your students' problem-solving and critical thinking skills. There are over 4,000 problems, sorted by topic and level, each of which is on a printable sheet with lots of room for students to show their work. Many are based on familiar themes, such as Harry Potter and summer vacation, that will capture the interest of first through eighth graders, and much of the material has been contributed by students. Don't miss the *Three Little Pigs* series, which takes kids through the familiar tale with math problems. They begin by figuring out the average age of the pigs, then progress through computing material costs for their respective houses, how hard the wolf has to blow to demolish each house, and finally the scrap value of the remains.

CHAPTER 9

VISUAL ARTS

See also Chapter 2—British History—Georgian England—Origins of Modern Childhood and Chapter 13—Warhol, Andy.

Art museums and galleries throughout the world have opened their doors to your students. Sit back and enjoy the world's greatest paintings, sculptures, photographs, textiles, and decorative arts with your class without worrying about keeping order and hushed reverence. We're sure these trips will inspire your students to take some of the online arts and crafts lessons included in this chapter.

ARTS AND CRAFTS CLASSES

Art Sparkers

http://www.arts.ufl.edu/art/rt_room/index.html

The Art Education Department at the University of Florida says that an "art sparker" is "an idea that excites the synaptic nerves in your brain and stirs your imagination," and they've provided 12 ideas to fire up your students' synapses—from drawing a family portrait to the art of camouflage. In the *@rtrageous* room, for example, students learn how to draw a family portrait, design wacky paper hats, or draw a cat by first learning how to physically act like a cat. Other areas of the tour include a section where students are taught how to think like an artist, a gallery with displays of student artwork (hosts explain how to submit your own works to the site), and the *@rtifacts Center,* which introduces your students to famous artists and art history.

Chinese Calligraphy

http://tqjunior.advanced.org/3614/Default.htm

The elementary school students who have designed this tour are anxious to teach your class the art of calligraphy. The tour begins with basic lessons on character and number formation and progresses to simple phrases. Along the way, students will learn some facts about China.

Drawing in One Point Perspective

http://www.olejarz.com/arted/perspective

Pay a visit to the cyber classroom of Harold Olejarz, artist and educator. Starting with basic tools and simple drawings, students progress to increasingly difficult one-point perspective sketches ranging from doors to televisions.

Origami

http://www.origami.vancouver.bc.ca

Among his other accomplishments, Mr. Joseph Wu was commissioned to do the origami versions of the "snowlite" mascots for the Nagano Olympics. Mr. Wu will take your students on a tour of origami art galleries and share his extensive knowledge of this ancient art form, including a history of paper folding and how to back coat and wet fold paper. During our visit we learned that the word *origami* comes from the Japanese words *oru* (to fold) and *kami* (paper). There are detailed instructions and diagrams for various origami figures, including sharks, seals, toads, and a jumping frog.

GALLERIES AND MUSEUMS

See also Chapter 2—Canada—Glenbow.

Akan and Yoruba Art

http://www.fa.indiana.edu/~conner/africart/

The University of Indiana presents this tour of Yoruba and Akan wood and metal art, a trip that also presents these two African cultures. The Akan of Ghana and the Ivory Coast make extensive use of a system of pictographic symbols, each of which is associated with a specific Akan proverb or experience. The pictographic writing is used extensively in textile, metal casting, woodcarving, and architecture. Included in this exhibit is a history of the people of the area, development of the crafts, and pictures of the artifacts. The texts tie art and culture together in ways that illuminate fascinating societal details. For example, the scales used to measure gold are not only beautiful objects, but their design makes it impossible to cheat.

Asian Art

http://www.asianart.org

This tour covers all aspects of Asian art through exhibitions, galleries, and articles. Because of its broad mandate, exhibits change frequently. During our last visit, we toured exhibits of Tibetan sculpture and calligraphy, works from Chinese artist Chaug Daichien (who has been compared to Picasso), drawings from the Himalayas, photographs of

Kathmandu, the material culture of the Tharu of Nepal's lowlands, Tibetan manuscript covers, Laotian textiles, and photographs of Mustang, known as one of "the last never never lands."

Caribbean Art Gallery

http://www.oir.ucf.edu/bryant

This purely visual tour of the William L. Bryant Foundation collection features the art and artifacts of Antigua, Aruba, Barbados, Curacao, Florida, Grand Cayman, Guyana, Haiti, Jamaica, Martinique, Puerto Rico, St. Croix, and Trinidad. Exhibits are filed by paintings, sculpture, fiber arts, household goods, and instruments.

Chesley Bonestell Art Gallery

http://www.bonestell.org/Page_1x.html

Chesley Bonestell was originally an architect who worked on major structures, including San Francisco's Golden Gate Bridge. At the age of 50, he began a second career as a motion picture special effects artist and worked on such famous movies as *The War of the Worlds*. This led to his third career as an artist. Bonestell is well known for his conceptions of outer space, long before the era of space exploration. This tour includes some of Bonestell's most famous paintings, as well as biographical materials.

Detroit Institute of Arts

http://www.dia.org

The fifth-largest fine arts museum in the United States presents paintings, sculptures, graphics, and decorative art from its many galleries. Check current exhibits, which regularly change, as well as archives of past exhibits such as *Ancient Art,* a tour of the ancient Mediterranean world that includes every artistic medium from the caves of Israel's Mount Carmel to gold artifacts from Ireland's Bronze Age. Other exhibits include master tapestry works from the late fifteenth to the early twentieth century, representing nearly all major European weaving centers, and *African Form and Imagery,* with more than 70 objects arranged according to function.

Diego Rivera Museum

http://www.diegorivera.com/index.html

Tours of the Diego Rivera Museum, with displays of his paintings and murals, are available in either English or Spanish. Although there is little textual information about the Mexican artist's work, biographical material is relatively detailed.

Escher, M. C.

http://www.worldofescher.com

Students will love the strange optical illusions of Dutch graphic artist M. C. Escher's works, several of which are displayed on this tour. There is also a collection of his quotes and anecdotes, many of which are as strange as his works. You might want to make sure that your students stay within the *Library* and the *Gallery* because other portions of this tour are highly commercialized.

Frederick R. Weisman Art Museum

http://hudson.acad.umn.edu

This tour of the Frederick R. Weisman Art Museum at the University of Minnesota features the works of Marsden Hartley, Alfred Maurer, and Georgia O'Keeffe. Be sure to check the temporary exhibits while you're there, which in the past have featured such topics as the art of maps; works of architects such as Ralph Rapson and Andrzej Piotrowski; and photographs by Dorothea Lange, Walker Evans, and Ben Shahn depicting the Great Depression.

Haring, Keith

http://www.haringkids.com

Keith Haring died in 1990 at the age of 31, but his whimsical pop art legacy still reverberates around the world. Kids will love not only his art but the story of his life as well. As a boy, Haring had a passion for drawing and found opportunities for creating public art everywhere, from subways to store fronts. His is also a story of rebelliousness, but always in the service of self-expression. (His biography does not avoid his sexual orientation or death from AIDS, so some may wish to avoid this part of the tour.) Haring believed that he could make any kid smile, and a visit to the Keith Haring Foundation's site is certain to brighten anyone's day. The tour includes a gallery of his works, as well as interactive activities that encourage art interpretation and creativity. For example, students are asked to write "who, what, and where" stories based on Haring's sketches. There are also lesson plans on drawing morphs and making flipbooks.

Los Angeles County Art Museum

http://www.lacma.org

This tour includes past and present exhibitions of artworks held by the Los Angeles County Art Museum, covering such areas as American art, ancient and Islamic art, costumes and textiles, decorative arts, European paintings and sculpture, Far Eastern art, photographs, prints, and drawings. The primary exhibitions lean toward the outré, such as German Expressionists' renditions of Old Testament art.

Museum of Modern Art (MOMA)

http://www.moma.org

Check the current exhibits and online projects at New York City's Museum of Modern Art, which frequently rotate among architecture and design, drawings, film and video, painting and sculpture, photography, and prints and illustrated books. Works are accessible by subject or through an alphabetical list of artists. Of special interest are the online projects that use the multimedia and interactive capacities of the Internet for art and art appreciation. For example, students can place various animated objects designed by artist Michael Craig Martin against different backgrounds, explore what happens when photographer Robert Cummings renders three-dimensional objects in two dimensions, or join MOMA's assistant curator as she travels to Japan, Russia, the Ukraine, and China to visit and interview local artists. There are also interviews with contemporary artists such as Coco Fusco, Gary Simmons, and Kara Walker, dealing with both their works and those held in the MOMA collection. Younger students will enjoy the *Art Safari,* which takes them on an exploration of animal artwork, and students of all ages will enjoy using digital images created by artist Peter Halley in which they are able to choose colors to illuminate areas of the image, print, and sign their finished compositions. The resulting work, which will bear Halley's signature, will be a collaboration between the student and the artist.

National Museum of American Art

http://www.nmaa.si.edu

The Smithsonian Institution's Museum of American Art houses an extensive collection of crafts, sculptures, photographs, paintings, and other works of art. There are over 3,000 digital images, accessible by subject or artist. Be sure to check the monthly feature and rotating online exhibits which, in the past, have featured the *Edward Hopper Scrapbook,* American poster art, and works by painter and printmaker Robert Cottingham. Those interested in photography will want to visit the *Helios Gallery,* which includes a collection of Civil War photographs by George Barnard and the *Matthew Brady Studio,* western landscapes by Timothy O'Sullivan and William Henry Jackson, and works by Clarence White and Gertrude Kasebier. Arts and crafts (including the famous White House Collection) are available for viewing in the *Renwick Gallery.*

National Palace Museum of Taiwan

http://www.npm.gov.tw

The National Palace Museum of Taiwan houses a varied collection dating back to tenth-century Northern Sung. Tours of the exhibitions and collections will give your students a detailed understanding of the history of Chinese culture through photographs and texts regarding the imperial collection—comprising calligraphy, paintings, books and documents, bronzes, porcelains, jade, lacquer ware, carvings, and tapestry. Be sure to visit the residence of Chang Ta-ch'ien, the famous Chinese painter and Buddhist monk. Tours are available in either English or Chinese.

Norman Rockwell Exhibition

http://www.rockwelltour.org

"The view of life I concentrate on in my pictures excludes the sordid and the ugly. I paint life as I would like it to be." The pictures in the Norman Rockwell exhibition center around four themes: *Inventing America, Drawing on the Past, Celebrating the Commonplace,* and *Honoring the American Spirit.* There are also a Rockwell biography; a family guide with games and exercises; and a teacher's guide with six lesson plans for high school students, which explore thematic and visual concepts as they relate to modern American society. Students can even send Rockwell postcards via e-mail.

Peabody Essex Museum of Art

http://www.pem.org/index.html

The Peabody Essex Museum of Art in Salem, Massachusetts, frequently changes exhibitions, but you can always count on something with a unique theme. When we last checked, the featured exhibit was *Odyssey: A Journey Into the World of Art,* which combined works from India, Japan, Zaire, and other countries with those by American masters John James Audubon, John Singleton Copley, Fitz Hugh Lane, and John Singer Sargent. Occasionally, the tours also include resources for teachers. During the release of the movie *The Crucible,* for example, middle and high school teachers could send away for a free curriculum guide covering the Salem witch trials.

San Francisco Fine Arts Museum

http://www.thinker.org

The San Francisco Fine Arts Museum may be the world's largest online collection, with over 75,000 objects from 12,000 artists. This tour features "Grid Pix" technology, which enables visitors to zoom in on the smallest parts of artwork to examine texture and minute details.

Web Museum

http://metalab.unc.edu/louvre

Join the 200,000 weekly visitors to the *Web Museum,* an extensive collection of famous paintings and biographies of hundreds of artists, from Paul Cezanne to Lewis Carroll. Tour by topic or artist, but please be cautioned that with the high visitation, navigation through this tour may be extremely slow.

World Art Treasures

http://sgwww.epfl.ch/berger/index.html

With so much to learn and so little time, you might want to consider a field trip that combines art and history lessons. Friends of Jacques-Edouard Berger—late curator of the Museum of Fine Arts in Lausanne, Switzerland, world-wide traveler, and art collector—have honored him by setting up the Jacques-Edouard Berger Foundation, which sponsors this tour. It interweaves a collection of great world art with Berger's own words and texts that attempt to place visitors back in time, as if they were experiencing the art when it was new. The last time we took the tour, there were 16 itineraries, including *Pilgrimage to Abydos,* exhibits on Vermeer and Botticelli, and a stunning exhibition of *Renaissance Gardens.* The exhibit *Shared Vision* covers several of the voyages that Berger made, and there is also a tour of the art of Southeast Asia, China, Japan, Europe, and India. Tours are available in English, French, Italian, and German.

NATIVE AMERICAN ART

See also Chapter 2—Canada—Glenbow.

Inter-Tribal Gallery

http://www.indart.com/gallery/gallery.htm

The *Inter-Tribal Gallery* contains a collection of paintings, sculpture, pottery, cultural items, beadwork, kachinas, and other works of art, primarily encompassing Native American tribes and artists from the Southwest. In addition to the varied and numerous works of fine and decorative art, there are links to Web resources for individual tribes.

Powersource Gallery

http://www.powersource.com/gallery/default.html

Powersource Gallery is a collection of Native American artistic symbols portraying "powerful people, powerful places, and powerful objects." In addition to works of art, there are texts on powerful places in Texas, New Mexico, and Arizona, as well as materials on ceremonial dances and powerful people. The *Powerful People* portion of the tour includes such historical figures as Cochise, Geronimo, and Sitting Bull (as well as lesser known Native Americans and such contemporary figures as Ben Nighthorse Campbell, the Colorado senator). Students may submit their own nominations via e-mail. Powerful Native American women are displayed in the *Woman Spirit* section and yes, Pocahontas is included in case your students are interested in learning the true story. (According to the tour, Wayne Newton, part Cherokee, is negotiating with England for the return of her remains.)

Santa Fe Museum of Indians

http://www.ou.edu/fjjma/studio/.index.html

The University of Oklahoma hosts this large display of southwestern Native American artists who paint in the "flat style"—seemingly primitive, with no background, but with a great attention to detail and ornamentation. More than a dozen Kiowa, Comanche, Cheyenne, and other artists' paintings are on display, with brief artists' biographies and discussions of their works. For additional paintings, follow the link to the Oscar B. Jacobsen collection.

Sisochi Gallery

http://www.yosemitegold.com/nativeamerican

This tour of Yosemite National Park's Sisochi Gallery focuses on Northwest Coast ceremonial masks and carvings; California baskets; Navajo war axes, drums, rattles; and works of art by contemporary Native American artisans.

PHOTOGRAPHY AND PHOTOJOURNALISM

See also Galleries and Museums—Frederick R. Weisman Art Museum, National Museum of Modern Art, and Museum of Modern Art, and Chapter 1—Civil War—Library of Congress Photographs and United States—National Archives and Records Administration.

American Museum of Photography

http://www.photographymuseum.com

The American Museum of Photography affords a perspective on the medium from its invention in 1839 through World War I. The photographs are from the personal collection of William B. Becker, a noted photography historian and broadcast journalist. Online exhibits have included Southworth and Hawes daguerreotypes, architectural photographs from 1845 to 1915, and 1866–1870 photojournalism. We suggest you begin with the guided tour, with its excellent textual overview of the current exhibits. If you get tired of looking at the photographs, check the *Research Center*, where various processing techniques and the preservation and protection of photographs are explained.

California Museum of Photography

http://cmp1.ucr.edu

The goal of the California University at Riverside's Museum of Photography is to "empower the visitor with an understanding of the critical role photography and related media have had in shaping both society and the daily lives of individuals." The tour is divided into three sections: *Exhibits*, *Collections*, and *WebWorks*. When we last checked, the tour included Matt O'Brien's documentation of the demise of the cattle

limitations and imperfections of technology, photographs taken by seniors, works by female photographers from the 1880s to the 1980s, images from the United States–Philippine War, the photographs of Herb Quick, burlesque portraits of Raoul Gradvohl, an exhibit of the hand-colored family pictures sold by traveling salespeople, the story of photographic backdrops, and a tour of the modern skate culture. *Collections* includes samples from the world's largest and complete holdings of vintage stereographs, one of the three greatest American public collections of cameras, historic photographs of California's 21 missions, turn-of-the-century images of Native American lifestyles and images, and quotes by Mark Twain. *Webworks* features exhibits conducted solely for the Internet, including the *Scanner as Camera* and Mary Flanagan's interactive display, which allows students to enter the "surrealistic world of her grandmother's dream state." We suggest you accompany your students on this tour because some of the exhibits, including guns, vivid images of a Cambodian prison camp, and nude photographs, may be considered inappropriate.

The Daguerrian Society

http://www.daguerre.org/home.html

The Daguerrian Society, founded in 1988, is an organization of individuals and institutions with an interest in the art, history, and practice of the daguerreotype photographic process. While browsing through the exhibits, you might want to download contemporary or period music, provided on site. The society provides several online galleries that display examples of daguerreotype collections, such as *Daguerreotypes in the Open* (an effort to document the changing face of a nation), *Reflections of an Era*, and *Modern Daguerreotypes*. Other information includes a history of the daguerreotype, an illustrated, step-by-step description of the process, and nineteenth- and twentieth-century texts.

Focal Point Photojournalist Group

http://www.f8.com

This tour, hosted by Focal Point, a photojournalist group, features real-time, online interactive photojournalism. For example, *Saigon on Wheels* details a journey through Vietnam's motorbike culture by *National Geographic* photographer Ed Kashi, and *Russian Chronicles* follows a 5,000 mile, two-month journey across Russia by photographer Gary Matoso and writer Lisa Dicky. With a high-resolution digital camera and laptop computers, Matoso and Dicky recorded their stories and relayed them to Focal Point via e-mail. The tone of many of the features will appeal to students. For example, in the feature on Cologne, Germany, photographers stop to interview teenagers. Conversely, teachers should be cautioned that some of the materials, such as profiles of life inside Brazil's infamous Candido Mendes penal institution, or portraits of landmine victims, can be rather disturbing.

George Eastman House

http://www.eastman.org

The George Eastman House in Rochester, New York, is a 12.5-acre museum on Eastman's former urban estate. It houses an extensive collection of photography organized around such themes as the history of photography (an interactive timeline allows students to travel as far back as 1725 to Johann Heinricks Schulze's discovery and experimentation with the darkening of light on a mixture of chalk and silver nitrate), a collection of daguerreotypes, early British and French photographs, nineteenth-century photographs of the American West, and works by Alvin Langdon Coburn and William Jennings. Samples from the organization's motion picture collections include videos of one of the first Lumiere brothers' films; a documentary of Edweard Muybridge; and an exhibit of toys such as the 1879 Reynaud "Praxinoscore Theatre," the precursor of motion pictures. Students can also learn about preserving photographs, from antiques to modern digital works. The curator will be happy to answer any of your questions via e-mail.

Smithsonian Photographic Library

http://photo2.si.edu

The Smithsonian archives contain hundreds of photographs covering a wide variety of topics. Exhibits include a salute to the cinema, a slide show of award-winning photographs taken by Smithsonian Institution photographers, underwater photographs, and various Washington, D.C., exhibits (cherry blossoms in bloom, the Washington monument, the Vietnam Veterans Memorial, etc.). Other exhibits cover fireworks (with information on the best way to photograph them), deadly Pacific sea snakes, lunar landings, the renovation of the First Ladies Hall, Kayapo Indian headdresses, butterflies, the jungle canopy of Panama, dinosaurs, Chief Justice Warren Burger's funeral, sea turtles in Costa Rica, what things are made of and why, and folk musicians.

CHAPTER 10

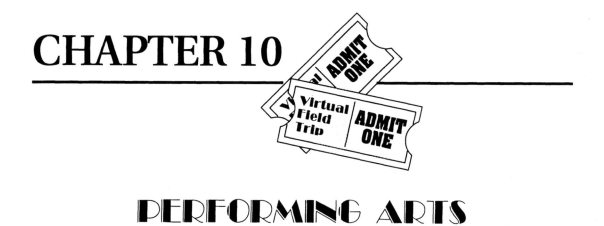

PERFORMING ARTS

From this year's Cannes Film Festival to Thomas Edison's early motion pictures, from Bach to rock, from classic opera to a world-wide cyberopera, your students can cover the history of dance, theater, music and movies. Along the way, they can learn piano, help create an opera, or attend world-wide cultural events, including hit plays, Balinese shadow theater, and kabuki. We've also provided tours of libraries with actual sheet music. Be sure to visit specific musicians in Chapter 13.

CINEMA

See also Chapter 9—Photography and Photojournalism—George Eastman Hosue and Smithsonian Photographic Library and Chapter 13—Wise, Robert.

Cannes Film Festival

http://www.festival-cannes.fr

Mingle with the rich and famous at the annual Cannes Film Festival. Students can take part in the red carpet ceremony, press conferences, photo sessions, and interviews. If you can't make it this year, don't worry about a thing. The events—from the 1940s to the current time—are archived on site. This is a must-see event for any serious student of film, or for those who simply like to indulge in casual star gazing and gossip. The hosts have provided access to all 50 plus years of the awards, including profiles of 22,000 attendees, 5,000 films, and 800 honors bestowed since 1946. They have also published news headlines of the time to give a perspective on world events and allow visitors to see the how the arts compare and contrast to historical and political events. For example, while the Nuremberg trial verdicts are being announced, the nation of Israel is being born, and the Marshall Plan is being implemented, Maurice Chevalier leads a parade through the streets of Cannes and Jean Paul Sartre strolls the Croisette in a bathing suit. Be sure to take a peak at the *Cannes Market* while you're there—usually only producers, sales, agents, distributors, and buyers are allowed.

Edison Motion Pictures

http://memory.loc.gov/ammem/edhtml/edmvhm.html

"I am experimenting upon an instrument which does for the eye what the phonograph does for the ear," announced Thomas Edison, as he invented the kinetograph (a motion picture camera) and the kinetoscope (a motion picture viewer). The experiments began in 1888 with work performed by Edison's assistant, William Kennedy Laurie Dickson, and in less than a decade films were available to mass audiences. (Edison was also responsible for producing films.) This Library of Congress tour features over 300 Edison films, from documentaries such as Admiral Dewey's landing at Gilbraltar to comedies and dramas, as well as a history of Edison's work with motion pictures, an overview of the various genres produced by his company, and the development and use of kinetophones and kinetographs. Either an MPEG or a Quick Time player is needed to view the films.

Silent Film

http://www.mdle.com/ClassicFilms

Students can travel back to the era of silent films in the United States and Great Britain courtesy of this Los Angeles-based silent film society, The Silent Majority. See film clips from silent movies currently showing at their Los Angeles theater, view their poster of the month, and spend some time in their gallery, with over 500 pictures of stars, directors, and scenes from silent movies. Current and past issues of their magazine, an index of filmmakers and performers, and lobby card displays are also available. We suggest you start with the guided tour for an overview of this extensive site and go back to any of the 13 sections for further details.

DANCE

Ballet for Beginners

http://www.geocities.com/Vienna/Choir/6862/

Even your non-dancing students can gain an appreciation for the skill and beauty of ballet on this field trip to a ballet studio. Animations, photos, diagrams, and clear, precise explanations not only cover the basic ballet steps but also many of the ideas behind this art form.

New York City Ballet

http://www.nycballet.com

The New York City Ballet is the only performing arts institution that trains its own artists, creates its own works, and performs in its own house. This tour will take students back to the origins of the institution, beginning with the original conception of Lincoln Kirstein to his collaboration with George Balanchine. There are a complete repertory, a trivia game, and bibliography. If there are questions that haven't been answered during the tour, the staff will gladly accept e-mail questions.

MUSIC

See also Chapter 13—Anderson, Leroy; Bernstein, Leonard; Classical Composers; Holiday, Billie; Mozart, Wolfgang Amadeus; and Wagner, Richard.

American School in Japan—Midi Music

http://iris.asij.ac.jp/music/MusicComp.html

The K–12 American School in Japan invites you to listen to original student musical compositions, some of which are the result of collaborations with students from around the world. American School students from over 35 countries composed, sequenced, and digitally recorded works in their Tokyo classroom and have provided instructions on how to listen to the music.

The Blue Highway

http://www.thebluehighway.com

A trip down the *Blue Highway,* from the Mississippi Delta to the blues clubs of postwar Chicago, will give your students an understanding of the cultural and social context of the blues. An eloquent introduction sets the tone for this journey, which includes visits with some of the genre's greatest influences, such as Robert Johnson, B. B. King, Willie Dixon, and John Lee Hooker. The hosts have thoughtfully provided a map of the highway and plenty of audio blues samples to listen to along the way. We suggest you supervise the trip and make sure your students stick to the highway and avoid diversions such as chat rooms and stores.

Classical Music Concert

http://metalab.unc.edu/wm/snd

Pay a visit to the *WebMuseum Auditorium,* with over a dozen classical compositions that can be enjoyed from the comfort of the classroom. The classical greats are well represented, from Mendelssohn's *Wedding March* to Beethoven's *9th Symphony.* This tour requires some supervision because there are links to Disney, Madonna, and other sites that may distract your students.

Composers in Electronic Residence (CIER)

http://www.edu.yorku.ca/ciermain.html

CIER, a joint project of Canada's York and Simon Fraser Universities, is essentially an interactive concert site, designed to enhance students' musical composition, performance, and appreciation skills. Student composers create and share original works using electronic MIDI files. Other students, teachers, and composers listen to the compositions on their own computers and share verbal and musical input, much of which results in original world-wide collaborative pieces. There is a slight fee for participation, although past works and dialogues, archived on site (available free of charge), also provide a valuable learning experience. Teachers should check the *How it Works* section for technical information.

Duke University's Digitized Sheet Music Project

http://odyssey.lib.duke.edu/sheetmusic

Now you can get your students into Duke University's Rare Book, Manuscript, and Special Collections Library to take a look at more than 3,000 pieces of sheet music from the eighteenth and early nineteenth centuries. The *American Sheet Music Project* is an invaluable resource for both music and history teachers and their students. The collection, classified by key word, date, and subject (classical, dance, education and fraternal organizations, entertainment, historical and patriotic, instruments, legacies of racism and discrimination, marches and military, sacred, United States society and culture, and vices), is composed of digital images of the original publications. Duke cautions people that, due to historical social norms, some of the materials, especially songs about minorities, may be considered offensive. There is an excellent overview of the definition of sheet music, a background on music publishing, publishing processes such as lithography and chromolithography, preservation, and the role of music in historical contexts and studies.

The Lester S. Levy Sheet Music Collection

http://levysheetmusic.mse.jhu.edu

The Lester S. Levy Collection of Sheet Music at Johns Hopkins University Library contains over 29,000 pieces focusing on popular American music from 1780 to 1960. Images of both the cover and each page of the music are available for those pieces published before 1923 (all of these items are also in the public domain). The strength of the collection lies in its documentation of nineteenth-century America, with particular emphasis on music reflecting military conflicts from the War of 1812 through World War I. The collection is searchable by topics, including minstrel, circus, dance, alcohol, temperance, smoking, presidents, romance, etc. Check *The Guide to the Lester S. Levy Collection of Sheet Music* for a full description of the 38 available categories.

1950s—Lucille's Rockin' Radio

http://www.integrityonline10.com/Lu/

Those who have Real Audio connected to their computers will want to tune in to *Lucille's Rockin' Radio.* This 1950s fan has compiled an extensive collection of the era's music, including doo wop, rockabilly, rhythm and blues, and gospel. Serious collectors should not miss the "rare" section of the site, with outtakes and unreleased recordings. You can listen to clips, view photos, and read detailed biographies of your favorite singers and groups from the 1950s.

Nineteenth-Century California Music

http://www.sims.berkeley.edu/~mkduggan/neh.html

The history of California—which is also the history of a dozen ethnic groups—comes alive through approximately 2,000 pieces of sheet music published in California between 1852 and 1900. It's a way to learn about history through commercial art (the sheet music illustrations are often beautifully and precisely detailed) and lyrics. The collection is searchable by culture, topic (including disasters, mining, politics, railroads, and sports), printer, art, dance, or theater.

Piano Lessons

http://library.thinkquest.org/15060

Sit back, loosen up your fingers, and prepare to learn how to tickle the ivories, courtesy of three high school students. There are 15 piano lessons, and the hosts have thoughtfully provided an on-screen piano for you to play. There are MIDI files so that you can hear what your piece should sound like, a glossary and encyclopedia, and composer and player biographies. The lessons cover rhythm, time signatures, and note reading. Once you feel confident, put yourself on stage at the virtual concert hall and play for anyone who happens to be in cyberspace. An interesting feature of this site is that your hosts not only allow but encourage you to contribute ideas and information to the site.

Rock and Roll Hall of Fame

http://www.rockhall.com

The greatest rock and roll performers, producers, and disc jockeys are hanging out at the *Rock and Roll Hall of Fame,* waiting to meet your students. Performers such as Chuck Berry, James Brown, and Eric Clapton are always ready to play some of their most famous songs for your students and share their stories. Those more interested in the business end may prefer to chat with legendary producers Sam Phillips and Berry Gordy Jr., or radio personalities such as Alan Freed. Others may prefer to tour the museum with Eddie the Elevator Man, who will give your students an excellent overview of the museum's permanent exhibits. Be sure to check the temporary exhibits, which frequently change. On our last visit, we learned about hip hop and Bob Dylan. The museum's curator is always available to answer questions. We suggest that you accompany your students on this tour and steer them away from the chat rooms.

Sounds from the Orchestra

http://tqjunior.advanced.org/5116

Listen to classical music while this student-designed tour teaches your students about the basics of an orchestra, its instruments, how sound is made, and what it looks like. Select the instrument of interest to hear sound clips and learn its history. There are even instructions for making your own musical instruments. We recommend this site not only for students interested in music, but for anyone who wants to see how students can design an intelligent, sophisticated Internet project.

 # OPERAS AND OPERETTAS

The Brain Opera

http://brainop.media.mit.edu

The Brain Opera exemplifies the power of the Internet to provide unparalleled educational opportunities. This cyberspace opera, created by Tod Machover and his extensive team of artists and scientists from the M.I.T. Media Laboratory, was composed entirely online by world-wide participants from all walks of life. Participants contributed rhymed couplets based on concepts and quotations from a provided story line. The results were then set to music and incorporated into a real opera, eventually performed in Austin, Texas. This tour allows students to attend the computer age performance of *Honoria in Ciberspazio*, centered around Rez, a writer and philosopher of virtual communities, and Sandy Stone, a cyberspace goddess.

Gilbert and Sullivan

http://diamond.idbsu.edu/GaS/index.html

The *Gilbert and Sullivan Archive* contains librettos, plot summaries, pictures of original Gilbert and Sullivan stars, scores, audio files, and articles about all 14 of the team's operas. This extensive tour also includes biographies, clip art, and a glossary. Students whose interest in the team may have been piqued by the film *Topsy Turvy* can find a link to the movie's site here.

New York City Opera Library

http://www.nycopera.com

Now you can bring your students to an opera library without worrying about inappropriate behavior. There are dozens of opera librettos, from classic to modern, with composer biographies and images from various productions. To spur interest in the subject, the hosts have included an online quiz. Answers can be found within the library's resources, and winners are announced on site.

New York Metropolitan Opera

http://www.metopera.org/home.html

If you want to instill a love of the opera in your students, don't miss this historic tour of New York's Metropolitan Opera. Begin in the opening season in 1883 and travel forward in time, witnessing such historical performances as Maria Callas as Lucia and Enrico Caruso's Samson.

RADIO AND BROADCASTING

Bellingham Antique Radio Museum

http://www.antique-radio.org/radio.html

Feel free to browse the collection of antique radio sets, speakers, microphones, and tubes at Washington's Bellingham Antique Radio Museum. Or, sit back and listen to comedies, dramas, world events, and advertising from the golden age of radio. The diverse choices include Edgar Bergen and Charlie McCarthy, Orson Welles's famous *War of the Worlds*, and speeches from historical figures such as Winston Churchill and Theodore Roosevelt. For those interested in electronics, Jonathan Winter, an old-time radio fan, has provided detailed multimedia instructions for building crystal radio sets, as well as historical textbooks such as the 1917 primer, *The ABCs of Electricity*.

SCRIPTS

http://script-o-rama.com

The extensive collection of television and movie scripts at this site covers a variety of genres, from current popular television series to classic movies. We suggest you supervise students during this tour, because unknown authors are allowed to contribute materials. However, if you stay within the television and movie categories, you will be more likely to avoid inappropriate material.

THEATER

American Variety Stage

http://memory.loc.gov/ammem/vshtml/vshome.html

The Library of Congress provides this multimedia exhibit of 1870–1920 popular American entertainment. The diversity of historical culture and social mores of the times is illustrated by the 334 English- and

Yiddish-language play scripts, 146 theater play bills and programs, 61 motion pictures, 10 sound recordings, and numerous photographs and items of memorabilia documenting the life and career of Harry Houdini. Teachers should be aware that many of the items in the collection contain rather risqué humor and ethnic stereotypes typical of the period. Administrators caution that searching the collection may be somewhat frustrating because of the "layers" that must be searched.

Balinese Shadow Theater

http://www.balibeyond.com/gamelan/wayangbali.html

Balinese shadow play, or *wayang kulit* (lit leather figures) is a combination of Indonesian and Indian ritual, lesson, and entertainment in which mythic tales are performed by shadows of hand puppets that are projected onto a screen. This tour will teach your students about the history of shadow theater, primary mythical figures, and Balinese instruments and music. There are also instructions on how to make the puppets and the required screen. It's rather sophisticated, so we recommend this tour for upper grades.

Kabuki Theater

http://park.org/Japan/Kabuki/kabuki.html

Bring your students behind the scenes of Kabuki theater, where they can learn the history and read about Ichimura Manjiro, a modern Kabuki actor. After they learn about the structure and how to put on makeup, bring them to the auditorium, where they can watch video clips of Kabuki performances and hear traditional musical instruments.

Miss Saigon

http://www.clark.net/pub/rsjdfg

Thanks to a pediatrician at the University of Maryland who is a *Miss Saigon* fan, your class can see scenes from the musical, meet performers, obtain the complete libretto, and view video and audio clips. There is also a study guide that deals with such topics as culture and conflict, the Bui Doi, and the Vietnam War. Of special interest is the section covering the creation of a musical through the study of the works of composers, set and lighting designers, critics, and actors.

Phantom of the Opera

http://borg.iea.com/~jemery

If you can't afford tickets, this is the next best option. In addition to pictures and sound clips, the tour includes a complete libretto, a biography of Gaston Leroux, a story summary, and a detour to the Paris Opera House.

Puppet Theater—Stage Hand Puppets

http://www3.ns.sympatico.ca/onstage/puppets

The goal of Stage Hand Puppets, a Canadian group, is to give children around the world an appreciation for the world of puppetry. Check the *Activity* page, where students can learn about the art of ventriloquism, obtain puppet patterns and paper puppets, and learn simple and complex hand shadows. We suggest you steer your students away from other sections of the tour, which are primarily an online catalog.

CHAPTER 11

LANGUAGE ARTS AND LITERATURE

One of the Internet's greatest achievements may well be the access it provides to libraries and great literary works. Whether you're interested in the classics, reference materials, speeches, poetry, special collections, or simply enhancing your students' vocabularies, you'll want to browse this chapter.

GRAMMAR, WRITING, AND VOCABULARY

Common Errors in English

http://www.wsu.edu/~brians/errors/

Send your advanced writers to Paul Brians's class. Brians is an English Professor at Washington State University, and he's compiled a list of hundreds of common and not so common errors made in the English language. Brians tells us, for example, that restaurants that list shrimp scampi on the menu are either "pretentious or clueless." It seems that scampi is the Italian word for shrimp, so what one is ordering in effect is "shrimp shrimp." Brians sets the record straight on some of his pet peeves, such as "assure" versus "ensure" versus "insure"; the confusion among "carat," "caret," "carrot," and "karat"; and the misuse of the word "decimate" (which does not mean "annihilate"). Lest one think that the professor is overly critical, he has also included a section of non-errors. Many of these include things that defy the way grammar has traditionally been taught. Brians tells us for, example, that it's okay to end a sentence with a preposition or to split an infinitive. Your ESL students will be interested in Brians's section on the most common English errors that speakers of other languages make.

Purdue University's Online Writing Lab

http://owl.english.purdue.edu/

A trip to Purdue's Online Writing Lab (OWL) offers your students resources to help them become more proficient writers. OWL offers advice and help with composition and grammar, as well as teacher resources and information about Internet search tools. Students can follow links to specific areas or use the on-site search feature. Kindergarten through twelfth grade teachers should check the resource section for lesson plans and ideas for working with ESL students.

Sounds of English

http://classweb.gmu.edu/classweb/swidmaye/sounds/sounds.htm

A trip to Sharon Alayne Widmayer's *Sounds of English* will benefit ESL students, speech pathologists and their students, and early learners. Widmayer, of the Education Department of Virginia's George Mason University, provides texts, pictures, and sounds to explain how to pronounce most of the vowel and consonant sounds in American English. Students simply click on a word to begin their language lessons. Widmayer has thoughtfully provided links to quizzes and further information.

Wacky World of Words

http://members.home.net/teachwell/index.htm

Word lovers of all ages will want to pay a visit to the *Wacky World of Words,* where hundreds of word puzzles and games make grammar, vocabulary, and spelling a fun and educational experience. Guess the mystery word of the week, play *Rhyming Buddies*, take an online spelling test, find words hidden within words, design original similies and oxymorons, and even combine words and math with *Fractured Fractions*.

Worldly Wise Word Games

http://www.hoadworks.com/gamemenu.htm

Are you tired of the traditional exercises used to enhance your students' vocabulary and verbal skills? Adrian Hoad-Reddick, an avid word puzzler and Canadian English, history, math, and computer science teacher, has provided dozens of word games that will challenge every student and teacher. Test your "collective sense" by choosing the appropriate word for groups of animals (e.g., a cete of badgers), play with animal verbs where one is able to "doggedly ferret out the answers," or work some "Lewis Puzzles," anagrams named after the creator, Lewis Carroll. Check the site often because new puzzles are constantly added. Hoad-Reddick has provided answer sheets so you can check your progress.

LECTURES AND SPEECHES

American Speeches

http://douglass.speech.nwu.edu/

Northwestern University, in Evanston, Illinois, invites your students to its Douglass Archives of American Public Address. The archives, named after Frederick Douglass, include dozens of speeches on major social and political issues in American history. From caring for the poor to women's rights, these are not the typical materials available in standard textbooks. Students will be able to read speeches such as "Why Women Should Vote" (Jane Addams, 1915) and "On Liberty" (John Winthrop, 1645). The speeches are organized chronologically as well as by speaker and issue.

PROSE AND POETRY

See also Chapter 13—Austen, Jane; Borges, Jorge Luis; Burns, Robert; Collins, Wilkie; Eco, Umberto; Faulkner, William; Fleming, Ian; Heaney, Seamus; Joyce, James; Rowling, J. K.; and Stein, Gertrude.

Atlantic Monthly's Poet Page

http://www.theatlantic.com/unbound//poetry/poetpage.htm

Publishers of the *Atlantic Monthly* magazine share audio and textual classical and contemporary poetry and essays. Students can listen to readings of the works of classic poets such as Shakespeare, Emily Dickinson, Robert Frost, Thomas Hardy, Ben Jonson, Walt Whitman, and William Butler Yeats. Contemporary poets such as Richard Wilbur also share their ideas and poems. For example, Philip Levine talks about politics, history, life, and why poetry matters, and Robert Pinsky reads excerpts from his translation of the *Inferno*.

Bartleby Library

http://www.bartleby.com

Spend some time browsing and reading great books at the *Bartleby Library*, named in honor of Melville's humble scrivener. The library provides works from hundreds of authors free of charge. Works, which include classic prose and poetry, fiction and nonfiction, are filed alphabetically by author, and reference books such as *Bartlett's Quotations* are also available.

Blake Archive

See also Chapter 13—Blake, William.

http://jefferson.village.virginia.edu/blake/main.html

This electronic archive, perhaps the most ambitious William Blake project ever attempted, is sponsored by the Library of Congress in conjunction with the University of Virginia. When completed, the archive will contain original copies of every one of Blake's books—many of which have never been reproduced—supplemented by paintings, drawings, and commercial illustrations. Eventually, the collection will contain approximately 3,000 images, indexed by subject, date, and theme.

Disney Storybooks   PG

http://asp.disney.go.com/DisneyBooks/StoryTime.asp

Disney stories can be read or heard at this site. Click on the cover of the book to select such illustrated Disney classics as *Bambi*, *The Jungle Book*, *The Lion King*, and *Pinocchio*. Teachers should be cautioned that there are many links to commercials for Disney products, so supervision may be necessary.

Favorite Poems Project

http://www.favoritepoem.org

Poet Laureate Robert Pinsky believes that the difference between silently reading and listening to poetry is like the difference between reading sheet music and listening to live musical performances. In his efforts to encourage the vocal expression of poetry, Mr. Pinsky created the *Favorite Poems Project*, where students are able to listen to various forms of the genre read by people from all walks of life. There are video presentations of readings ranging from Bill Clinton's rendition of Emerson's "Concord Hymn" to a Massachusetts construction worker's presentation of Walt Whitman's "Song of Myself." Pinsky also provides suggestions for organizing poetry readings in your local schools and communities.

Grandad's Animal Alphabet Book

http://www.maui.com/~twright/animals/htmgran.html

Kids can learn the alphabet in English or Spanish with *Grandad's Animal Alphabet Book*, an electronic primer developed by Thomas Wright for a computer graphics course. Mr. Wright has 16 grandkids, and his primer provides an animal and poem for every letter of the alphabet (the Xuprocar is an animal from another planet). After exploring the various letters of the alphabet and learning about animal classifications, your students can test their knowledge with an online quiz, which will be scored automatically. Students can read the materials on their own or follow along with the audio.

Nineteenth-Century German Stories

http://www.vcu.edu/hasweb/for/menu.html

Bob Godwin-Jones, from the Humanities Department of Virginia Commonwealth University, invites your students to stop by for an evening of late eighteenth- to nineteenth-century German literature. Jones has compiled the narrative works of several German authors, many with original illustrations. English and German translations are shown side-by-side, and many of the works, which include Wilhelm Busch's *Max and Moritz* and the tales of the Grimm Brothers, have glossaries and dictionaries.

The Ovid Project

http://www.uvm.edu/~hag/ovid/index.html

The University of Vermont's Rare Book Department owns an extensive collection of the illustrated works of Ovid. Included are several editions of *The Metamorphosis,* with engravings by the seventeenth-century German artist Johann Wilhelm Baur, depicting 150 scenes. Each engraving has a brief description in German and Latin and is accompanied by English text. Some plates from a 1640 edition of the translation, done by George Sandys, are also available.

The Shiki Internet Haiku Salon

http://mikan.cc.matsuyama-u.ac.jp/~shiki/

Doesn't it make sense to take your students to Japan to learn to write haiku? Named for Masaoka Shiki, a haiku master whose name means "four seasons," this tour offers explanations of this poetic form, said to be the shortest in the world, and step-by-step processes for writing your own. Learn about past and modern haiku masters and read winning entries from the last few international contests.

Treasures from the Saxon State Library

http://lcweb.loc.gov/exhibits/dres/dresintr.html

The Saxon State Library was founded in 1556 when Prince Elector Augustus started a formalized system of acquiring books and literary works. Until 1990, the library's holdings were behind the Iron Curtain and thus virtually inaccessible. Now your students can take a tour of the great exhibitions of engraving, incunabula, bookbinding, and design that stretch from medieval and Renaissance times through Goethe. The online collection includes a series of detailed texts on the history of the Saxon State Library and its various holdings, including a copy of Luther's translation of the Bible, the thirteenth-century text "Moses and the Ten Commandments," an early Latin gospel, a Boccaccio, and many other medieval and Renaissance manuscripts. Texts are accompanied by richly detailed graphics of cover pages and other illustrations.

221B Baker Street

http://www.sherlock-holmes.co.uk/home.htm

Grab your magnifying glass and pipe and head to *221B Baker Street,* where the folks at the Sherlock Holmes Museum will show you every room inside the fabled flat. To help put your students into the proper mood, they can listen to music from the BBC *Sherlock Holmes* television series during their tour. There are also texts of some of the favorite Holmes stories, and a newspaper story about the East End murders, one of the many cases that proved to be merely elementary for the great detective.

CHAPTER 12

SPORTS AND LEISURE

Perhaps a day at the circus, a game of chess, or a relaxing day in a girls' clubhouse is in order. For those who are still running on high rpms, perhaps a day of extreme sports or a visit to the Indy 500 is in order. If not, send them to Alaska for the Iditarod, and be sure to tell them to write.

CHESS

http://chess.liveonthenet.com/chess/archive.html

British philosopher R. G. Collingwood believed that a person becomes a master in chess once he believes that he will always be a beginner. Beginners and masters will all benefit from a visit to the *Chess Archives.* Like the game itself, this tour will satisfy every level of complexity. Beginners can study opening moves, follow a complete match with explanations for every move, study endgames, or analyze some of the greatest chess matches in history.

CIRCUS   `PG`

http://www.ringling.com/education

Step right up and enjoy the front row seats that Ringling Brothers Circus has reserved for your class! The online activities include a tour of the Circus Hall of Fame, where students will be introduced to such notables as lion tamer Gunther Gebel-Williams, master clown Lou Jacobs, and, of course P. T. Barnum. The hosts will tell your students about all of the circus animals—from alpacas to zebras. Others may prefer to visit the *Awesome Arcade,* where they can play educational games or create a clown. If you're thinking about running away to join the circus, make sure you take the online aptitude test to see which jobs you would be most qualified for. Other quizzes of varying levels of difficulty also test your knowledge, and the ringmaster is happy to accept e-mail. A special section for primary grade teachers includes activities such as clown face sandwiches, stilt walking, and role-playing circus games.

CLOWN HALL OF FAME
http://www.clownmuseum.org/mainpage.html

Hop on board the rolling calliope and fling a pie! The folks at the Clown Hall of Fame in Milwaukee, Wisconsin, want you to appreciate the art of clowning, which dates back to ancient Greece. Students will learn the art of clown make-up and how to distinguish between white face, auguste, and character clowns. Learn about the long, glorious—and not always funny—history of clowns. All of the greats are here, including Red Skelton, Emmet Kelley, and Peggy Williams—the first female graduate of Ringling Brothers and Barnum & Bailey Circus's Clown College.

GIRL'S WORLD
http://www.agirlsworld.com

Described as "the space where girls rule the place," this site is conceived as a clubhouse where girls are able to band together to boost their self-esteem and get some advice from their peers. Materials are written and edited solely by girls and teens and include frequently updated profiles of famous and everyday girls; recipes; crafts; advice on friendship, boys, family, careers, and tough issues; a list of pen pals; fun facts; and even "tricks" to play on boys. For example, you can bet a boy that you can predict the score of a baseball game before it even starts (zero to zero, of course). New members are encouraged to join (free of charge) via the on-site registration form, and site administrators insist that no last names or identifying personal information will be given out. However, if you prefer not to register, all materials with the exception of "chat rooms" are still available. Despite the advertising (you may want to steer your students away from the *mall*), a trip to this site is worthwhile and topical. Girls can seek advice on such issues as "how to get the boys in class to clean up their acts," how to get their moms to let them be more independent, and how to feel safe in school. Check the site to see how you can become a *Girl's World* writer or editor.

JUGGLING HALL OF FAME
http://www.juggling.org

"I do six plates and bounce the ball on forehead after ten years of practice, and people just say, 'It's good'," laments Hall of Fame juggler Massimiliano Truzzi. Meet world-class jugglers in the *Juggling Hall of Fame*. It's a select group indeed. Qualifications are quite stringent; to even be considered for membership, a juggler must possess special artistic or technical skills. Inductees include Enrico Rostelli, who is noted not only for juggling the most balls (10), but for his technical skills; W. C. Fields, perhaps the world's greatest comedic juggler; and Truzzi, who said that, "Life requires a human being to understand both philosophy and juggling, because it takes a little of both to get along in the world today."

MR. ROGERS' NEIGHBORHOOD   `PG`
http://www.pbs.org/rogers

It's a beautiful day in the neighborhood, so why not take your kids to visit Mr. Rogers? He will share the words to his favorite and most familiar songs, take you on a tour of his house, and take you to the land of make believe. There's a lot to keep youngsters busy, including fun facts and show-and-tell.

PROFESSOR BUBBLES' BUBBLESPHERE   `PG`
http://bubbles.org

Professor Bubbles, who has appeared on television shows and concerts world-wide, will show you his bubble inventions and how to make your own bubble tools from everyday items like pieces of hose or hangers. He'll also share his recipe for the ultimate bubble solution and teach you the history of bubble blowing. You'll learn about the Pear Soap Company in England, which popularized bubbles in the nineteenth century.

RAINY DAY RESOURCE PAGE   `PG`
http://www.cp.duluth.mn.us/~sarah

If you want to keep your students occupied during indoor recess, have them pay a visit to this site, where they will find recipes for play dough (both edible and inedible), bubbles, oobleck, etc., and instructions for making paper airplanes, pine cone bird feeders, and more.

SPORTS

Automobile Racing
http://www.indy500.com

It's usually difficult to get tickets to the world's longest single-day sporting event. But now you can take your students on a tour of the famous Indianapolis 500 Motor Speedway courtesy of the World Wide Web. Go back in time to the track's initial conception by Carl Fisher in the early 1900s and participate in major historical Indy events. You'll want to get to know some of racing's notables, beginning with the winner of the first race, Ray Harroun. Harroun averaged 74.6 miles per hour and would no doubt be amazed at speeds achieved in later years. There are also a three-dimensional tour of the track, racing statistics, and a press room with transcripts of past Indy events.

Dog Sledding

http://www.sleddog.org

The Alaska Dog Mushers' Association will teach your students all about the sport of dog sledding, and your class can listen to broadcasts of actual races. There are even tips for your first race (don't forget your snow hook and sled bag).

http://www.iditarod.com

In 1925, Nome, Alaska, was threatened by a diphtheria epidemic. The nearest serum was 674 miles away, and 20 dog sledding teams made the trip in 1,275 hours, saving the city of Nome. This event is commemorated in the annual Iditarod race (known as the last great race on Earth), which begins in Anchorage each year on the first Saturday in March. Modern Iditarod racers now make the 1,200 mile trip in 10 to 12 days. Why not take your students to the next race? Current and former participants will show them how to read maps and teach them the official rules, which cover both sportsmanship and care for the dogs and the environment. If you still have the energy, you may want to hang around Nome for a while and attend a reindeer potluck dinner and see some of the local sites.

ESPN

http://espn.go.com/sportscentury

Go back in time to New York's Ebbett's Field in 1938, when Johnny Vander Meer was the first to pitch three consecutive no-hitters. Discover how the 1908 middleweight champion Billy Papke was responsible for referees instructing boxers to "shake hands and come out fighting." Be there as Michael Jordan became the first player in 1988 to score at least 50 points in consecutive NBA playoff games. Each day, ESPN highlights great moments in twentieth-century sports, and each week another top athlete is inducted into their list. There are greats from all of the sports, including Secretariat, the first animal to be signed by the William Morris Agency for guest appearances. All will be inspired by athletes such as Lou Gehrig, who never called in sick in 14 years (he played 2,130 consecutive games).

Gymnastics

http://www.gymn-forum.com

Current and past gymnastics greats are all hanging around the *Gymn Forum*, and they'll be happy to tell you all about themselves and the world of gymnastics. Be sure to visit the *Gymnastic Centurions*, including Bart Conner, Frank Comisky (known as the master of the pommels), and Dominique Dawes. You can even take an online gymnastics trivia quiz.

Jump Rope Federation

http://www.usajrf.org

The United States Jump Rope Federation will keep your students apprised of the latest news in the world of jump roping. Each quarter, a new jump rope skill or topic is featured, with photographs, animations, and text. This section of the tour is for the advanced athlete and features complex techniques such as a combination double under, 360, and outside leg tuck. The less adventuresome can spend their time in the photo gallery or reading about featured jumpers and teams. Teachers may want to steer their students away from the product advertisements.

National Basketball Association

http://www.nba.com

Despite the heavy advertising during this tour, there's a lot of free, interesting information to be gained from this tour hosted by the NBA. Some of the most renowned players and coaches are always available to talk about the greatest moments in basketball history, techniques, rules, and officiating. Students can learn about the history of the game and keep apprised of the latest news. If you time your visit correctly, there may be an NBA member conducting a live chat.

National Hockey League Players' Association

http://www.nhlpa.com

The National Hockey League Players' Association (NHLPA) has created this family-oriented tour. In addition to the standard statistics, current scores, and standings, the players' biographical materials include childhood photos and quotes from their parents. For those who have always felt that ice hockey is a frantic free-for-all, a glance at actual sketches from playbooks will bring home the strategies and intricacy of the sport. Students can test their own hockey strategies and plays with the NHLPA web animator.

Sports Illustrated for Kids

http://www.sikids.com/index.html

Archives of past stories from *Sports Illustrated for Kids* cover a variety of topics, including interviews with professional athletes, things athletes do for good luck, and tips from professionals. Electronic polls ask such questions as, "Is there too much stress on teenage tennis pros?" Fun features include photographs, jigsaw puzzles, opportunities for students to e-mail their questions (sample question: "Why isn't women's pole vaulting an Olympic event?"), and pictures for which kids can e-mail their own captions.

STREET CENTS

http://www.halifax.cbc.ca/streetcents

This tour is the online companion to the award-winning Canadian Broadcast Company's television series, which primarily teaches kids to be smart consumers. Each week, a new topic is covered and added to the archives of the site. Learn why CDs are cheaper at some places and how to obtain dreadlocks or book bags at the best price. Your students can also watch live videos with teenagers discussing issues of relevance such as curfews and school uniforms.

THOMAS THE TANK ENGINE   PG

http://www.thomasthetankengine.com

Thomas and his friends are waiting for you at the engine shed. While they're resting and getting washed, stop in at the waiting room and play some memory games, work puzzles, and do some math problems. Be sure to visit the ticket office gallery, where there are coloring pages (you can even paint online) or, if you prefer, design your own Thomas Web page. Teachers may want to steer their students away from the *Sodor Store*.

CHAPTER 13

PEOPLE YOU SHOULD KNOW

Tired of waiting for someone famous to visit your school? Then take a trip to meet a famous person, unhampered by agents, press secretaries, managers, or long lines. Historical figures, authors, poets—they're all waiting to teach and entertain your students.

AFRICAN AMERICANS IN THE SCIENCES
http://www.princeton.edu/~mcbrown/display/faces.html

Louisiana State University invites your class to this exhibit, which profiles African American men and women who have contributed to the advancement of science and engineering. There are dozens of biographies of scientists, doctors, mathematicians, and inventors, complete with pictures and bibliographies. The materials are arranged alphabetically by last name and discipline.

ANDERSON, LEROY
http://www.leroy-anderson.com

Leroy Anderson's orchestral miniatures, such as *Sleigh Ride*, many of which were arranged by Anderson for the Boston Pops Orchestra, are some of the best known American concert music pieces. Students can listen to various Anderson works while perusing a photo gallery, brief biographical materials, and a discography.

AUSTEN, JANE
http://www.pemberley.com/janeinfo/janeinfo.html

In addition to compiling almost everything Austen ever wrote—from novels to poems and letters—this tour includes biographical materials, scholarly articles, pictures of the Austen family, a map of England showing Austen landmarks, links to other Austen resources, and even a list of the top Jane Austen songs based on the characters in her novels. Administrators admit that they're obsessed with Austen, but it's a magnificent obsession. You can even join discussions about movie adaptations of Austen works.

BERNSTEIN, LEONARD
http://www.leonardbernstein.com

In 1943, with less than a day's notice, a 25-year-old composer made his debut with the New York Philharmonic Orchestra. Students can attend the appearance, which catapulted Leonard Bernstein to fame. This official site covers the life of Bernstein through letters, photographs, concert programs, scores, telegrams, working notes, and other materials. During the tour, students will also have the opportunity to get to know Bernstein's family, friends, and colleagues such as Aaron Copeland, and listen to clips of some of his most famous works, such as *Candide*, *On the Town*, and *West Side Story*. The tour allows students to search for a specific media type or tour Bernstein's studio, which includes photographs of his piano and scores from his personal library.

BLAKE, WILLIAM
See also Chapter 11—Prose and Poetry—Blake Archive.

http://members.aa.net/~urizen/blake.html

Richard Record, a computer programmer and William Blake enthusiast, wants to introduce your students to the works of the famous author. In addition to the complete text and color plates of *Songs of Innocence* and *The Marriage of Heaven and Hell*, there are a dozen of Blake's paintings, including *Satan Inflicting Boils upon Job*, and extensive biographical materials and articles addressing how Blake's poetry and art were inextricably entwined.

BORGES, JORGE LUIS
http://www.themodernword.com/borges

Borges, the linguistic illusionist, would love this site, which pays homage to the man, his thoughts, and works. In addition to the biographical materials one would expect, there are images of the Argentinean author that have been "tweaked" to create surreal effects and a generous selection of Borges quotations. (One of our favorites is his comment on a translation: "The original does not do justice to the translation.") There are selections from his works, including several that have never before been translated from Spanish.

BURNS, ROBERT
http://www.robertburns.org

Students can meet the famous Scottish poet at this site, with a selection of biographical materials, songs, and poems. There is information about the people Burns knew and the places he lived and visited, as well as detailed instructions for hosting a Burns' Supper on the traditional date of January 25. To help you communicate with Robbie, the site provides a glossary of Scottish terms.

BUSH, GEORGE AND BARBARA
http://bushlibrary.tamu.edu

Some of the important events that occurred during George Bush's presidential term included the end of the Cold War, the beginning of democracy in eastern Europe, the passage of the Americans with Disabilities Act into law, and the reunification of Germany. The George Bush Presidential Library and Museum at Texas A&M chronicles these events and the lives of George and Barbara Bush. Follow Bush's career through his service at the United Nations, the Central Intelligence Agency, Congress, and the presidency. Materials include his major speeches (organized chronologically), an extensive collection of photographs, biographies of Bush and his wife, and information on Barbara Bush's Foundation for Family Literacy.

CARTER, JIMMY
http://carterlibrary.galileo.peachnet.edu

Take your students to downtown Atlanta for a tour of the Jimmy Carter Library and Museum. Electronic holdings include Carter's daily presidential diary, photographs, speeches, and biographies of Carter and his wife Rosalynn. Of particular interest is the exhibit on the Camp David Accords, which outlines the diplomatic history leading to the meetings and discusses the preparations necessary for hosting the meetings, the daily negotiations, and their impact on history. There is a special *Kids Corner*, as well as exit interviews with members of Carter's administration, including Zbigniew Brzezinski, Lloyd Cutler, and Stuart Eizenstat.

CLASSICAL COMPOSERS
See also Chapter 10—Music.

http://voyager.physics.unlv.edu/webpages2/picgalr2.html

The *Classical Composers Archive* contains dozens of portraits, each accompanied by biographical information. Composers can be selected either alphabetically or by their nationality.

COLLINS, WILKIE
http://www.rightword.com.au/writers/wilkie

Only on the Internet would you travel all the way to Australia to visit a minor Victorian writer. Wilkie Collins, a contemporary and friend of Charles Dickens, wrote a series of stories and novels in the genre then known as "sensation fiction." Today, the works would be classified as a combination of detective and horror fiction. The hosts of this tour will share information about Collins and some of his best-known works (*The Woman in White* and *The Moonstone*) and illustrations from his books.

DA VINCI, LEONARDO
http://www.leonet.it/comuni/vincimus/invinmus.html

Pay a visit to the Leonardo da Vinci Museum and show your students what a Renaissance genius could do. Tour the east wing to see his oil paintings, including, of course, the *Mona Lisa* and *The Last Supper,* and the west wing to view reproductions of Leonardo's engineering and futuristic designs, with accompanying text. Your students will certainly be interested in how a man born centuries before the Wright brothers designed a helicopter. The north wing has additional da Vinci drawings and sketches, and the south wing has information on Leonardo's life and the times in which he lived.

DAVIS, JEFFERSON
http://www.ruf.rice.edu/~pjdavis/

Jefferson Davis, president of the Confederacy, was also a Mexican War hero, a member of both the House of Representatives and the Senate, and President Franklin Pierce's Secretary of War. Rice University has published several of Davis's letters and speeches, as well as biographical information and photographs, excerpts of which are available at this site.

DE TOCQUEVILLE, ALEXIS
http://www.tocqueville.org

"I sought the image of democracy itself, with its inclinations, its character, its prejudices, and its passions, in order to learn what we have to fear or hope from its progress." In 1831, the 25-year-old Alexis de Tocqueville embarked on a nine-month tour of America, sent by the French government to study the American prison system. Students can follow his journey, courtesy of C-Span. There are journal entries; letters; biographical materials; and lesson plans dealing with issues such as religion and politics, the power of the press, and the role of government.

DICKENS, CHARLES
http://www.fidnet.com/~dap1955/dickens

Travel back to Victorian England and spend some time with Charles Dickens to learn how his early life is reflected in his works. He'll be leaving for a period of time in 1842 to travel and comment about some of the major cities in America. (He finds Philadelphia handsome, "yet distractingly irregular.") The Dickens page also talks about his illustrators and links to sites with copies of his works.

ECO, UMBERTO
http://www.themodernword.com/eco

Meet the Italian author of fiction, essays, academic texts, and children's books. Eco, a professor of semiotics at the University of Bologna, is known for his playful use of language, symbols, and puzzles and his narrative inventions. Students can view biographical materials, summaries of reviews of his works, quotes, and photographs of the author.

EISENHOWER, DWIGHT DAVID
http://www.eisenhower.utexas.edu

The Dwight D. Eisenhower Library and Museum highlights the memorable events that occurred during Eisenhower's term of office. It was during this time that the Department of Housing, Education, and Welfare was created; the Korean War ended; the Geneva Accords were signed; the historical *Brown v. Board of Education of Topeka* decision was made; federal funding for the construction of interstate highways was established; the 1957 Civil Rights Act was passed; both *Sputnik* and *Explorer I* were launched; and Alaska and Hawaii became states. Feel free to wander through the site, viewing primary and secondary multimedia source materials.

FAULKNER, WILLIAM
http://www.mcsr.olemiss.edu/~egjbp/faulkner/faulkner.html

Mississippi honors its native son with commentaries, plot synopses, a biography, a filmography, trivia, quotations, and a glossary. There is a personal welcome from the great author himself, and part of the tour takes you through his fictional Yoknapatawpha County.

FLEMING, IAN
http://www.mcs.net/~klast/www/fleming.html

Take a tour of this site and you'll see why the creator of the James Bond novels was John F. Kennedy's favorite author. The tour includes photographs, biographical materials, articles, and interviews, as well as Fleming's personal library and the site of his grave. Learn the truth about Fleming's rumored connections to the CIA.

FORD, GERALD
http://www.lbjlib.utexas.edu/ford/

Pay a visit to Michigan's Gerald R. Ford Library and Museums in Ann Arbor and Grand Rapids. In addition to over 300 historical photographs of the president and first lady, students will see an impressive collection of documents from the Ford presidency. Primary source materials include declassified pages of National Security Study and Decision Memoranda compiled by Brent Scowcroft, minutes of cabinet meetings, and speeches such as the Nixon pardon and Ford's inaugural address. Be sure to tour the *Day in the Life of a President* exhibit, a reproduction of Ford's daily diary with links to documents, photographs, and video clips. Ford begins his day at 6:50 in the morning, and before his day ends just past midnight he has posed for photographs with Miss National Teenager and ordered the evacuation of the last American troops from South Vietnam.

4,000 YEARS OF WOMEN IN SCIENCE
http://www.astr.ua.edu/4000WS/4000WS.html

This tour is the result of a series of speeches given by Dr. Sethanne Howard, currently of the National Science Foundation. The hosts at the University of Alabama tell us that women have been active in science as long as we have been human. Although the first scientist recorded in literature was male (the architect of the pyramids), the second, En Hedu'Anna, a woman who studied the moon and the stars, lived 4,000 years ago. Your students can meet all of these diverse women, from Maria Agnesi, whose Witch of Agnesi curve still appears in today's textbooks, to the actress Hedy Lamar, whose original idea and patent led to modern cellular phone technology. The concept of "science" is placed in historical perspective as the hosts explain that it was formerly a part of natural philosophy, a field encompassing grammar, rhetoric, logic, mathematics, music, and astronomy. Students who tour the *Hall of Fame* and answer the quiz correctly get their own names entered in the hall.

FULLER, BUCKMINSTER
http://www.thirteen.org/cgi-bin/bucky-bin/bucky.cgi

Buckminster Fuller, the captain of "spaceship Earth," is best known for his geodesic domes. This colorful 1960s architect, designer, engineer, poet, philosopher, and author was one of the first people to be involved in the ecology movement. Materials at this site, which include interviews and pictures of Fuller domes, are from a television show funded by the National Endowment for the Humanities and the National Endowment for the Arts with American Express corporate sponsorship. There are interviews, textual material, and photographs.

HAYES, RUTHERFORD
http://www.rbhayes.org

The Rutherford B. Hayes Presidential Center in Fremont, Ohio, houses the nineteenth president's former home, as well as a library (the first presidential library) and museum. In addition to biographical materials, students can tour some of the rooms of the Hayes mansion and view primary source documents and photographs.

HEANEY, SEAMUS
http://metalab.unc.edu/dykki/poetry/heaney

Heaney is deemed by some to be the most important Irish poet since William Butler Yeats. Your students will be able to make their own decision after touring this multimedia site covering the 1995 Nobel Prize winner's life, poetry, and speeches.

HOLIDAY, BILLIE
See also Chapter 1—African American History—Encyclopedia Britannica's Guide to Black History.

http://users.bart.nl/~ecduzit/billie.htm

Follow the 25-year career of one of the world's greatest jazz singers, as she transforms from Eleanora Fagan to Billie Holiday to Lady Day. In addition to biographical materials, there are music clips, bibliographies, discographies, lyric sheets, and Holiday portraits. This comprehensive tour even includes Holiday's FBI file. **Note:** This site is slated to change its address soon. If you can't find it at the above URL, try *www.ladyday.net.*

HOOVER, HERBERT
http://www.hoover.nara.gov

Herbert Hoover lived through some of the most exciting and harrowing times in history: the Roaring Twenties and the War on a Thousand Fronts. The Herbert Hoover Library and Presidential Museum opened on the eighty-eighth birthday of the thirty-first United States President, known throughout the world as the "Great Humanitarian." The facility has over seven million pages of document holdings, a generous sample of which are available on this tour. There are detailed biographical materials covering Hoover's life and the events of the eras during which he lived; a teacher curriculum guide; and a special section for K–8 students where they can view a collection of political cartoons, learn how to play "Hooverball," and take an interactive quiz.

JEFFERSON, THOMAS
http://www.monticello.org

How would you like to spend an entire day with Thomas Jefferson? You'll have to begin early, because Jefferson has had a lifelong habit of rising out of bed the minute it is light enough to see the hands on his clock. Enjoy the views and historical artifacts throughout the various rooms at Monticello or accompany Jefferson as he participates in his usual activities: reading, writing, eating, and visiting. Wait until you see his inventions, such as the "clothes turning machine," a kind of precursor to the moving racks in today's dry cleaner shops. At the end of the day, Jefferson dies (on July 4) and his epitaph, per his request, mentions the three things he considered to be his greatest accomplishments: writing the Declaration of Independence, composing the Virginia Statutes (concerning religious freedom), and founding the University of Virginia.

http://lcweb2.loc.gov/ammem/mtjhtml

The Manuscript Division of the Library of Congress provides a collection of primary source documents pertaining to Thomas Jefferson. Become acquainted with Jefferson through his correspondence, drawings, financial account books, and manuscripts from 1806 to 1827. Students can follow Jefferson through his activities as president of the United States, as a delegate to the second Continental Congress, drafting of the Declaration of Independence, as governor of Virginia and a congressman, and as minister plenipotentiary to the court of Louis XVI.

JOHNSON, LYNDON BAINES
http://www.lbjlib.utexas.edu

Lyndon Baines Johnson wanted young visitors to his library and museum to "achieve a clearer understanding of the presidency and . . . a clearer comprehension of what the nation tried to do in an eventful period of its history." Multimedia exhibits include *America from 1908–1973* (covering Johnson's childhood in Texas; his careers as congressman, senator, vice president, and president; the 1960s; the War on Poverty; civil rights; Vietnam; and the Great Society), gifts of state, oral history transcripts, photographs, and recordings of some of Johnson's presidential telephone conversations.

JOYCE, JAMES
http://www.2street.com/joyce

Your students can hear Joyce reading passages from *Finnegan's Wake* and hear the actual song that gave Joyce the title. There are articles, maps, a biography, photographs, complete texts of major novels, an electronic journal devoted to Joycean scholarship, the landmark Supreme Court decision ruling that *Ulysses* was not obscene, information on joining a Joyce electronic mailing list, and a list of actual non-cyberspace James Joyce reading groups.

KENNEDY, JOHN FITZGERALD
http://www.cs.umb.edu/jfklibrary/index.htm

The stated purpose of Boston's John Fitzgerald Kennedy Museum and Library is to "advance the study and understanding of Kennedy's life and career and the times in which he lived; and to promote a greater appreciation of America's political and cultural heritage, the process of governing and the importance of public service." This tour includes speeches made by John, Robert, and Edward Kennedy; biographical materials; quotations; a photo gallery; digital copies of Kennedy-Khrushchev correspondence; audio and visual transcripts of the Kennedy-Nixon debates; digital copies of correspondence from civil rights leaders such as Roy Wilkins, Whitney Young, Dr. Martin Luther King Jr., and John Lewis; and primary source documents regarding the Cuban Missile Crisis and Americans in space.

KING, DOCTOR MARTIN LUTHER, JR.

See also Chapter 1—African American History and United States—1968.

http://www.stanford.edu/group/King/

Stanford University's extensive collection of primary and secondary materials is the result of a long-term collaborative effort with the Martin Luther King, Jr. Center for Nonviolent Social Change. The collection, which includes biographies, articles, and King's speeches, is intended to "clarify the nature and source of his ideas and leadership style." Upon completion, the collection will comprise 14 volumes. Visitors may register free of charge to keep apprised of updates to the site.

MANDELA, NELSON

http://www.pbs.org/wgbh/pages/frontline/shows/mandela

This tour is based on the PBS *Frontline* television program, *The Long Walk of Nelson Mandela*. His life as a boy, revolutionary, prisoner, husband, and leader is explored through interviews with Mandela and his friends and enemies, political allies, and fellow prisoners. An excellent teacher's section provides an historical overview of South Africa, and poignant discussion questions and activities explore such issues as apartheid, compromise, nationalism, leadership, and conflict resolution. For example, students are asked to compare the life of a Black American and a Black South African.

MARQUEZ, GABRIEL JOSE GARCIA

http://www.themodernword.com/gabo

Speaking of his fellow Latin Americans, Nobel Prize-winning, Colombian-born author and Mexico City resident Gabriel Garcia Marquez says, "To oppression, plundering and abandonment, we respond with life." Now students can become acquainted with Marquez, one of the pioneers of magical realism, through biographical materials (including a detailed history of Colombia) and a gallery of photographs, paintings, and book covers. The materials are frequently updated to include the author's latest works.

MCCARTHY, JOSEPH

See also Chapter 1—United States—Adrian Scott and the Hollywood Ten.

http://webcorp.com/mccarthy

Beginning with the timeless quote from Santayana—"Those who cannot remember the past are condemned to repeat it"—this tour takes your students back to the 1950s era of McCarthyism, where they can hear some of the senator's speeches and, hopefully, gain new appreciation for the principles of democracy. In addition to photographs and McCarthy's speeches, students can hear the words of the Council for the Army that effectively ended the era—Welch's famous, "At long last, sir, have you no shame?"

MEADE, GEORGE

See also Chapter 1—Civil War.

http://adams.patriot.net/~jcampi/welcome.htm

Through primary and secondary source documents, students can learn about the multi-faceted Union Civil War Major General George Gordon Meade (1815–1872). In addition to standard biographical materials, there are letters and reports written by Meade, his admirers, and his critics. Of particular interest is the controversy over the Gettysburg campaign, when Meade permitted Confederate solders to "escape" across the Potomac River.

MONROE, JAMES

http://monticello.avenue.org/ashlawn

Students can visit with James Monroe at his Ash Lawn-Highland estate, where he resided from 1799 to 1826. The tour through the estate's grounds and various rooms includes displays of such articles as a watch belonging to Mrs. Monroe and the couple's bed, complete with trundle board. There is a brief Monroe biography and description of Ash Lawn-Highland as a working plantation. The interesting history of Ash Lawn-Highland explains as much about the young United States as about the property. The estate was adjacent to Jefferson's property, and when Monroe went overseas as an ambassador, Jefferson arranged to have the orchards planted. In Monroe's later years, his wife become ill, his finances became strained, and he was forced to sell the property.

MOZART, WOLFGANG AMADEUS

See also Chapter 10—Music.

http://208.4.223.8/lecagot/mozart.asp

Visit with the great Austrian composer, while listening to his music, courtesy of an Internet radio broadcast from Spain. Be sure to spend some time in the portrait gallery, with dozens of paintings of Mozart, and read some of the biographical materials. We were especially interested in the collection of Mozart's letters. In one, begging for money, he writes, "I have been obliged to resort to the moneylenders; but as it takes some time to seek out the most Christian among this un-Christian class of people, I am at the moment so devoid of funds that I must beg you, dearest friend, in God's name, to support me with however much you can spare. If, as I hope, I get the other money in a week or two, I will immediately repay what you lend me now—as to what I have owed you for so long already, I must ask you to continue to be patient."

MUIR, JOHN
http://www.sierraclub.org/john_muir_exhibit

The Sierra Club invites your students to meet the great naturalist, John Muir. We suggest you prepare for this trip by downloading the K–12 teacher's guide. Begin your tour with the quote of the day from Muir and then visit the gallery with photographs, drawings, and woodcuts produced by Muir; his writings; geography cards that explain the connection between Muir and various parts of the world; movies; songs about Muir; people instrumental in his life; and an extensive bibliography.

MURPHY, AUDIE
http://www.audiemurphy.com

World War II hero and movie star Audie Leon Murphy won every decoration for valor that the United States had to offer, as well as five medals from France and Belgium. Richard Rodgers, a high school teacher concerned that memories of Murphy are fading, has established this site, tracing the life of the most decorated soldier of World War II from his impoverished Texas childhood (his mother cooked everything extra spicy so the kids would feel full on less food) through the war and into Hollywood. Rodgers also offers 44 still shots and captions of the autobiographical movie, *To Hell and Back,* which Murphy starred in. (Murphy also wrote the book.)

NIXON, RICHARD M.
http://webcorp.com/video/nixon

There may not be a U.S. president, including Lincoln, who made more famous speeches than Richard Nixon, although they are remembered for quite different reasons. Now your students can hear some of Nixon's most memorable speeches, such as the famous "Checkers" speech, his "last press conference," and comments made during Watergate. This tour takes a rather cynical view of Nixon, so you may wish to balance it with other materials at the Nixon Library: *www.nixonfoundation.org.*

POLK, JAMES J.
http://www.jameskpolk.com

This 1816 Federal-style home is the only surviving residence of the eleventh president. Tours of James J. Polk's ancestral home include a biography and a tour hosted by C-Span (a Real Audio player is required). We recommend that teachers check the *Educational Resource* section for grades K–12 lesson plans and activities.

PRINCE OF WALES

See also Chapter 2—England—British Monarchy.

http://www.princeofwales.gov.uk

Despite his busy schedule of approximately 500 public visits each year, the Prince of Wales has set aside time to mingle with your students. Through his Web site, the prince wants to know your views on various issues of importance to him. When we last checked, he wanted to know how the Commonwealth could change to better meet the needs of its members. He's also deeply interested in environmental preservation. The tour also includes an archive of his speeches, copies of his public diary, his official biography, and a picture gallery. While your students are mingling with royalty, they can listen to the royal harpist.

PULITZER PRIZE WINNERS

http://www.pulitzer.org

This tour affords students the opportunity to meet current and past winners of the prestigious Pulitzer Prize, honored for their excellence in journalism, letters, drama, and music. What a gathering! All of the winners (searchable by name or date) from the award's inception in 1917 will be there. See the past five years' winning photographs, editorial cartoons, music clips, and full-text articles. While you're there, stop in and meet Joseph Pulitzer.

REAGAN, RONALD

http://www.reagan.utexas.edu

This site is still under construction. However, a tour of the *Ronald Reagan Presidential Library* currently includes biographies of Reagan and his wife Nancy and a selection of historical photographs.

ROOSEVELT, FRANKLIN

See also Chapter 1—United States—New Deal Era.

http://www.fdrlibrary.marist.edu

Presidential libraries exist largely because of Franklin Delano Roosevelt, who was instrumental in the passage of the act that made presidential materials the property of the public. Previously, presidential papers were the property of the individual and their distribution and/or disposal was left to chance. Pay a visit to the Franklin Delano Roosevelt Library in Hyde Park, New York, to learn about Roosevelt and his family and view exhibits from his life, from his 1884 christening dress to his grave. There is a searchable database of FDR speeches and papers, as well as a link to the FDR Museum, which features people and events instrumental to his presidency.

ROSS, BETSY
http://www.ushistory.org/betsy/index.html

The story of Betsy Ross is one of triumph over adversity. During this tour, students will learn how Mrs. Ross overcame exile from the Quakers and the loss of three husbands and two infant daughters. They will also be able to read the story of how she sewed the first American flag, take a tour of her house, and even learn how to cut a five-pointed star in one strip—she taught George Washington the same skill. There is also information about the flag, including flag etiquette, trivia, and a photo gallery. Do you know who was the only person in history honored for cutting the American flag into pieces? Visit Betsy and she'll tell you all about it.

ROSSETTI, DANTE GABRIEL
http://jefferson.village.virginia.edu/rossetti/index.html

Thanks to the University of Virginia, your students are able to visit an exhibit of the complete works of Dante Gabriel Rossetti (1828–1882), the pre-Raphaelite poet and painter. There are images of his manuscripts, early printed texts and proofs, drawings, paintings, and biographical materials. Rossetti will open his studio to your class—the virtual tour is so detailed that there are even sketches pinned on the walls.

ROWLING, J. K.
http://www.angelfire.com/wi/harrypotter

Get the very latest news about J. K. Rowling and Harry Potter, where rumors are debunked, facts verified, and updates furnished. Students can get the inside information on unreleased books and the movie and send e-mail owls to people at Hogwarts. They're also encouraged to write their own Harry Potter stories, read others' submissions, or take the Quidditch trivia quiz. Have your students check out the riddles section, which reveals the mythological sources for Rowling's names, and learn the real secret of the Mirror of Erised (hint: spell "erised" backwards). Everything you'll want to know about Harry's friends, enemies, and the Hogwarts faculty is here.

STEIN, GERTRUDE
http://www.tenderbuttons.com

The goal of this tour is to introduce new perspectives on Gertrude Stein and make new materials on her life and work available online. Pleasingly designed, with graphic logos appropriate to Stein's works (*Very There, Go Ask Alice*), the site comes equipped with a critical annotated bibliography, a quarterly journal, and links to Stein scholarship. However, the site is still in development and not all the links are currently fully functional. Stein enthusiasts should definitely pay a visit, and the site also looks promising as an introduction to those unacquainted with this brilliantly experimental writer.

TESLA, NIKOLA
http://www.neuronet.pitt.edu/~bogdan/tesla

Bogdan Kosanovic, a Ph.D. in electrical engineering, has put together this homage to the man who held over 500 patents on such inventions as fluorescent lights, AC power transmission, rotating magnetic fields, the induction motor, and the radio. Visit Tesla in Niagara Falls, New York, and at the 1893 Chicago World's Fair, as he displays his latest inventions. He will share his views, occasionally acerbic, on everything from Edison to science. The collection of Tesla anecdotes includes his boyhood experiment with wings. He stood on a roof, hyperventilated until he felt light headed, and then jumped.

THOMAS, GEORGE HENRY
See also Chapter 1—Civil War.

http://home.att.net/~dmercado

Explore the life of Major General George Henry Thomas (1816–1870), known as the "Rock of Chickamauga." Among his other accomplishments, Thomas was Commander of the Army of the Cumberland during the Civil War—he had chosen to side with the Union at the expense of being disowned by his sister and his home state of Virginia. Thomas was one of the few senior Union officers possessing extensive field experience with artillery and cavalry armaments, but despite his many victories, he never achieved the ranks of Civil War heroes. Students will be able to explore Thomas's relationships with Generals Grant, Sherman, and Schofield—all of whom became three-star generals at the expense of his reputation. There are also trivia questions (don't worry—there are hints), photographs, and biographical materials.

TRUMAN, HARRY S.
http://www.trumanlibrary.org

Long before the concept of the sound bite, Harry S. Truman's colorful sayings ("If you can't stand the heat, get out of the kitchen") captured world-wide attention. Best known for his controversial decision to drop the bomb on Hiroshima, the thirty-third president of the United States had a long and colorful life (1884–1972). The 18,000-square-foot Harry S. Truman museum captures his personality through photographs, original documents, and biographical materials. Special exhibits include the Truman Chryslers, World War II, NATO, the creation of Israel, education modules, and a link to *Project Whistlestop,* a special tour for grades 1–3.

WAGNER, RICHARD

See also Chapter 10—Music.

http://users.utu.fi/hansalmi/wagner.spml

Hannu Salmi, a Wagner scholar, will introduce your students to the famous German composer. In addition to biographical materials and primary source documents, students will be able to listen to Wagner's works. One of the interesting features of this tour is the collection of articles written by Wagner, which cover a wide range of topics, from his theories of opera to his opinions about politics.

WARHOL, ANDY

http://www.warhol.org

This tour includes a representative sample of the more than 3,000 Andy Warhol works of art, as well as tapes and biographical materials held by Pittsburgh's Warhol Museum. Your students can tour the facility floor by floor or check the exhibits currently on display.

WISE, ROBERT

http://www.afionline.org/wise/robert_wise.html

The American Film Institute will introduce your students to the filmmaker Robert Wise, director of such classics as *West Side Story, Sound of Music, The Day the Earth Stood Still*, and *Star Trek: The Motion Picture*. Through biographical materials, photographs, movie synopses, and film clips, students can follow Wise's career, from the 1940s, when he received an Academy Award for editing work on *Citizen Kane,* to films of the 1980s.

WRIGHT, FRANK LLOYD

http://www.swcp.com/flw/tourthenat.html

Let the Frank Lloyd Wright Conservancy introduce your students to the famous architect and some of his most notable works. You will be able to tour the country and view such Wright-designed buildings as the Guggenheim Museum in New York and houses in Wisconsin and Illinois.

INDEX